My Guide to Million Dollar Months

*A Proven Client Acquisition Strategy
for Coaches & Consultants*

Krista Mashore

My Guide to Million Dollar Months

A Proven Client Acquisition Strategy for Coaches & Consultants

Krista Mashore

Published by Game Changer Publishing

Paperback ISBN: 978-1-962656-38-2
Hardcover ISBN: 978-1-962656-39-9
Digital: ISBN: 978-1-962656-40-5

www.GameChangerPublishing.com

Foreword

If you take a bunch of amazing people and put them in a room, someone will emerge as **excellent**, even among already excellent folks. Recently, I did just that. I brought Krista Mashore into my high-end, high-achieving, Driven Mastermind ($25,000 per attendee). These are the brightest of the bright, and they sat at the feet of Krista and listened, attention rapt, taking notes with glee.

Krista is **supra**-excellent, not just as a businessperson but also as a friend. We instantly clicked when a mutual acquaintance (Steve Harward) connected us less than a year from this writing. Krista had studied private trainings I did for a business group selling over one billion dollars of product collectively and was working through it and applying it and wanted my eyes on it. In the book, you'll see part of what makes Krista an outstanding teacher - she is an outstanding student.

The higher up you go in business, the bigger the egos get. Krista is a refreshing exception to that. She is one of the smartest, sharpest, and most sincere minds I know in business, yet she constantly learns, implements, and improves. I was honored to give her insight into my specific areas of expertise and excited about how she took it, ran with it, and made it hers. As I watched, I *learned*. She made me better.

I want you to imagine two mirrors pointed at each other. Each mirror has an image of its unique value. As these mirrors reflect their values off each other, the value multiplies. That's how I feel about Krista. Her values and how she shows up bring out the best in others, which she receives to enlarge her value, which brings out even more in others, ad infinitum.

If one million dollars a month sounds like a lot, consider a penny. One single cent that doubled its output daily (1, 2, 4, 8, etc.) would only need twenty-one days to exceed one million. Krista will help you uncover your value - whatever it is today - and help you multiply it far beyond what you can imagine now.

– Jason Fladlien, *known as the quarter billion dollar webinar man*

Foreword

Have you ever met someone who lights up the room? Someone whose energy is so captivating that you can't help but feel uplifted? That's Krista Mashore! In the vast world of real estate and coaching, where dreams are both made and broken, Krista shines brighter than most.

I'm Dean Graziosi. Over the decades, I've worn many hats – entrepreneur, multiple NY Times bestselling author, and co-founder of Mastermind.com with my dear friend Tony Robbins. Together, we've orchestrated some of the most monumental virtual training events in history.

On this journey, I've had the privilege of meeting numerous talented individuals, but Krista stands out. Why? Because she doesn't just succeed; she elevates everyone around her. Whether on stage or behind the scenes, Krista isn't merely present—she is a dynamo. She isn't just a participant; she is a driving force. She doesn't just make sales; she makes genuine, lifelong impact.

Flashback to July 2022, and I confess I hadn't even heard of Krista Mashore. Tony Robbins and I were immersed in the launch of an all new revolutionary product. We rallied influential affiliates and friends in the Self Education industry—names like Brendon Burchard, Russell Brunson, Jenna Kutcher, Ed Mylett, and hundreds more—who all united to magnify our message.

Yet, amidst this galaxy of renowned talent, a name emerged atop the leaderboard. A name that bore the weight of the underdog narrative, an element I've always held a special fondness for. That name… Krista Mashore!

Watching Krista rise was a spectacle of fire and determination, defying odds and leaving heavy hitters in her wake. But let's dig a bit deeper. Krista's story isn't just about accolades, numbers or sales. It's about heart. It's about the underdog in her who never gave up, the coach in her who sees potential in others, and the go-getter who knows how to turn dreams into realities.

Now, she's pouring all that experience, wisdom, and passion into this book. She wants others to grow their businesses and expand their reach so that more people out there can get the help they need. As you dive into these pages, Krista isn't just sharing her journey; she's inviting you to embark on yours.

Based on her tried and tested strategies, she provides invaluable insights. And while no book can guarantee overnight success, embracing Krista's wisdom will undoubtedly steer you closer to your goals. So, here's to the journey ahead, to the lessons we'll learn, and to the success we're about to achieve, together.

Stay eager, stay inspired,
– Dean Graziosi.

Table of Contents

Introduction

You've picked up this book, and maybe you're thinking, *A million dollars per month from a coaching business or high ticket offer? That's impossible!* Nope, it isn't.

I started out in 2017 with absolutely no coaching clients and zero income from coaching. All I had was a burning desire to coach other people so they could find the success in real estate that I had found. I took classes and joined masterminds. I sought out experts and picked their brains. And then, I just started with what I had and what I knew to build my business. I kept tweaking what I was doing and tracking the results, making plenty of mistakes along the way. In less than three years, I was bringing in a million dollars per month consistently and we've recently done $4 million in a month.

And now I'm teaching others to do it. Of course, people don't typically make $1 million in the first month, and the results people get depend on how much effort they put into it. That said, a brand new student of mine who teaches a certification class in a specific type of hypnosis just did over $103k in his very first month. Another student who worked with multi-level marketers did $108k in his first month despite having technical issues during his training. They were able to do that because they followed the Million Dollar Month Model (MDMM) that I've created. They succeeded because they used a model that is replicable and repeatable. So, I'm going to ask you to keep an open mind. You can learn it and model it, too.

I'm sure you've seen parts of this model where people present virtual events to attract people into their programs (usually some kind of free webinar followed by a longer 2-3 day training where they make their offer). It might even look easy to you to just slap together a presentation and put it out online. But the Million Dollar Month Model (MDMM) is not just doing webinars or events. It's a complete client acquisition and conversion framework. It's everything that you do before, during, and after that gets people to say "yes" to you. It's exactly what you do at the virtual event and what you say at the virtual event. It's the stories that you tell. It's the text messages and emails that you send as reminders and encouragement. It's the funnels that nurture prospective clients and get them to convert. It's all these things put together that make this model work. The good news is that it's an art and a science that you can learn.

You may think that you have to be super extroverted and a natural salesperson or a really good speaker to build a great coaching business. That's not really the case. You just have to know how to present information in an influential way so you can attract people and show them how much you can benefit their lives. And as long as you're sincerely enthusiastic about what you offer, even if you're an introvert, you can still do a great job persuading people to join you, right? A lot of people have hang-ups about "sales," and being a good salesperson can even be considered sleazy. I'll talk more about *ethical persuasion*—helping people to say "yes" to what they really want and need—in Chapter 1.

My students and I didn't succeed because we are smarter or better than you. I'm no genius, and I didn't start out with all the advantages in life. I'm going to share my story with you because we all have limiting beliefs about what we can or can't do based on who we think we are. When you hear about how I started out, I'm guessing you'll think, *Oh, my gosh! If she can do this, so can I!* See, I'm the girl who wet her bed till she was 10. I'm the girl who had severe learning disabilities, and I wasn't able to read until the 4th grade. In 2nd grade, I was put in a special education class for three years. I'm the girl who ended up in juvenile hall, then a group home, and then in foster care. I'm the girl who hasn't lived at home since I was 13.

And I'm the girl who was abused by a parent.

Before I get into my story, I want you to know that I am very, very close to both my mom and dad. My dad is one of my best friends. My mom is the most loyal, loving person ever. But my mom had her own childhood challenges that affected the way she raised me. My biggest passion is to help people and to make a true impact on the world. I had to show them where I came from, that I was just like them. When I realized this, I wrote my mom a letter on a yellow piece of paper. I was crying, asking my mom if it was okay that I shared what had happened to me as a child. I didn't want her to be hurt, and she's done a lot to help me with my healing over the years. I love her. She has done everything she can to help heal my wounds and help me continue to grow.

See, as a child, it was almost like I lived in two families. We had a very happy, loving family. Yet underneath, I experienced physical abuse that only my mom and I knew about. By the time I turned 13, I couldn't handle it anymore. I started running away from home. I lived in abandoned buildings. I lived in my friend's parents' RVs. I lived in friends' closets at night while their parents were sleeping, and the parents had no idea that I was there.

Eventually, my parents or the police would always find me. I'd run away again. They'd find me. I'd run away again. I just couldn't handle the abuse anymore. This went on for over a year. I cannot describe to you all of the scary experiences I found myself in during that year. To this day, I know that I truly had a guardian angel by my side, keeping me safe from the real bad guys out there. I truly believe those angels protected me so that one day I could help others who have had issues (which is *all* of us!), and so I could be a catalyst of hope and inspiration to help others find the happiness and fulfillment we all deserve. (By the way, in this book, if I talk about guardian angels or the Universe or God and your beliefs are different, please don't let the words get in the way of the message!)

Finally, one day, I broke the law. My best friend and I broke into my eighth-grade PE locker room and stole all the girls' clothes and their lunch money because we had no food and no clothes. We got caught. My best friend and I were sent to juvenile hall. When we got there, I remember thinking, *I don't belong here.* I remember seeing this girl with bright red hair who was like six feet tall! I watched her grab another girl's head in the bathroom and slam her head into the porcelain toilet. Blood was gushing everywhere. And I remember thinking to myself, *I'm going to die in here. I don't belong in this place. I'm going to die here.*

I spent three and a half months in juvenile hall. When I finally got out, I was sent to a group home for troubled girls in Cottonwood, California. Every day, we would get dropped off for school in this big, green bus that had "Hidden Hills Group Home for Girls" plastered all over it. That bus announced to the rest of the school, "Hey, we're screw ups. We're trash. Don't talk to us. Ignore us, make fun of us." It was a horrible year. High school is a pretty crucial time when just about everybody feels insecure and vulnerable, right? Well, every day when I got dropped off on that bus, I felt like a total loser! It was just another blow to my confidence, one more thing that made me feel unworthy and "less than." It's a feeling I carried with me for many years until I learned to deal with it. The thing is that it never completely disappears. You have to continually face and battle those feelings.

I stayed in the group home for a year. I ended up becoming a peer counselor, one of the youngest teen counselors that they had ever had. Then I got sent back home. Though the physical abuse had stopped, things had not changed. There was so much history, so much that was unspoken, so much the rest of my family didn't know about, I realized I had to go.

So, I called my probation officer and I told him I needed to leave. My dad didn't understand what was happening. I remember him standing on the driveway, begging me not to leave. "Krista, we love you. Whatever it is, we can work it out. Please stay, please don't go." I was sobbing. My dad was crying. I couldn't tell him why I had to leave, and he didn't know about the history between my mom and me. He worked so hard to support us and to be a good father. (Later, I found out the only time he had ever cried was when his mom died and when I left home that day.) I was so sad having to leave my brothers and my parents. And I loved my mom, but I just couldn't stay there.

While my foster dad drove me to my new home in his silver Toyota truck, I cried the whole way. I cried myself to sleep for months. Even today, when I speak of it, tears come to my eyes, just as they are right now as I am writing this. I spent the next three years in a foster home. When I turned 18 and graduated from high school, my foster parents kicked me out of the house because the money quit coming in. They had been good to me, but I couldn't expect them to take care of me forever. The statistics for foster kids who end up on drugs or homeless after the State stops paying for their upkeep are crazy! I had to get very resourceful, getting loans and working all day so I could go to school at night.

When you go through physical abuse from a parent, it is psychologically very damaging. As a kid and even as an adult, a lot of crazy stuff can go on in your head about it and what the abuse says about you as a person. It's taken a lot of work on my part to believe in myself, to break out of that cage, and to believe that I'm worthy and deserving of love and deserving of good things.

When I got out of the foster home, I went through a lot of counseling. I remember sitting in my family's driveway because I wanted to ask my mom to tell the family why I had left. My leaving had caused a horrible ripple effect. My mother went through a lot of pain because of the memories that she had suppressed from her own childhood that came up during the years of my absence. The family was a wreck once I left. I felt as though my brothers blamed me for it, which made me feel even worse about myself. I wanted the family to know the *real* reason I left was not because I wanted to be wild, crazy, and free.

I sat in that driveway for a few hours crying, fearful about confronting her. Finally, I got the courage to confront her. "Mom, I need you to tell Dad what happened. He thinks I left because I just wanted to party. I need you to tell him why I really left." Mom was nothing but amazing. It was hard for her, but she went to counseling with me. She admitted what she had done, and it helped me heal. And she told the whole family so the family was able to heal.

Today, after a start in life that was pretty tough, I own a business that generates over a million dollars per month. If I could come to where I am with all those odds against me, whatever you've got against you can also be overcome.

Just a couple of years ago, Mom broke down crying. It was like one of those heart-wrenching scenes in a movie. She was balled up like a baby, crying so hard that she couldn't stop for hours. She was so upset that we had to call a close friend who was like a second son to her to calm her down. The pain of what she had done was overwhelming her. "I'm so sorry for what I did to you. I feel so guilty."

I told her, "Mom, I would not change my childhood for anything." And I mean it. I don't want her to feel guilty about it at all. Everything that happened to me made me who I am and made it possible for me to help as many people as I can today because it makes me more relatable and aware of limiting beliefs people have that can hold them back—just as everything that has ever happened to you has contributed to who you've become and can help you make a positive impact on others. I'm grateful, in a way, for all the things my life has brought me. No regrets and no guilt. (By the way, guilt is one of the most useless emotions that we carry. It just holds us back and keeps us stuck in negative feelings.) Forgive yourself, be better, and move on!!

My success at building my coaching business is not because I'm naturally gifted or that I had a great start in life. It's because I'm passionate about what I do, and I have developed a system that truly works. After my first couple of years using the Million Dollar Month Model (MDMM), I was asked to teach it at Russell Brunson's Inner Circle. To be a part of the Inner Circle, everyone paid between $50,000 and $250,000, and they had to have created a funnel that generated a minimum of $1MM in sales. To be a presenter at that group, you definitely have to know what you're doing at a very high level.

But did I start that way? Heck, no!

Let me tell you about my very first virtual event. When COVID hit, I was already coaching. But though I seemed to be doing well, my business was at a six-week burn rate because my expenses were way too high. Plus, I had just lost two of my key people and my entire sales team! I had to completely change the way that I was doing everything, right? I wasn't doing virtual events, and because of COVID, everything shut down, so I couldn't do live events. It forced me to have to do virtual events. I didn't know how to do virtual events, but I saw Tony Robbins and Dean Graziosi start doing them. I knew I had to just start. I just had to take some kind of imperfect action to keep my business from going under.

I just did it with Zoom when I started, and that first time, I think, 40 people showed up. I remember feeling like, *Oh my gosh, this sucks. Nobody's here!* But I had to make the decision that I was going to act like there were 400 or 4,000 people and just go for it and give the same quality I'd give to a huge audience. It was great because I learned a lot. Then I did it again two weeks later, and we had a couple hundred people show up because we got better at what we were doing. The thing is, I had no choice. We all had to pivot. Not everyone did, but I saw the big names doing it, and those were the people I knew I needed to emulate. I just had to start, and I had to be willing to adjust and modify and adapt as I went along. This was when I started developing the Million Dollar Month Model.

Of course, in the very beginning, I had all the same questions and concerns everyone has. Not that many people really knew me in the coaching field yet. I'd never done a virtual event before. What if I bomb? What if nobody buys from me? I had all those thoughts. I didn't have a big team, so I was running the virtual event myself with just one team member. Yes, it was hard at first, but it got easier, and we just kept making it better and better.

The reason I'm telling you all this is to let you know that no matter what you believe about yourself, you can do this. You can create the coaching business or high ticket offer that you've always wanted. You can step up and use your knowledge to make a great impact on lots of lives. All you have to do is have a little faith and follow the model, the Million Dollar Month Model.

CHAPTER 1

Unleashing Your Million Dollar Month Mindset

I built my coaching business from literally zero income and no students to consistently generating Million Dollar Months in just three years. In this book, I'm going to show you all the incredible strategies and techniques I used to do that. It took me thousands and thousands of hours and literally over a million dollars to learn these strategies. I've seen them work for me and work for my students, so they can definitely work for you, too.

But you know what? Strategies and techniques are *not* what's going to get you where you want. Why? ***Because you'll never build the coaching business or high ticket offer business you want if you don't get your mindset straight.*** I'm not exaggerating. I've learned this from my years coaching entrepreneurs. Early on, I started out all eager to give them every awesome strategy I knew. But I quickly realized that when I focused on coaching them on their mindset *first*, students were *much* more successful. They had fewer strategies at first than my first students, but they were crushing it and getting results much faster.

Mindset is the key in every business at every level. I've spent at *least* as much time and money working on my own mindset as I've spent learning great business-building strategies. And I continue to work on my mindset daily because I know how crucial it is. Shaquille O'Neal once said: "Of course, you have to have a little bit of talent—but if you have a certain mindset, nothing can stop you." The way I say it to my students (and I say it over and over): ***"Mindset trumps skill set every time!"***

If I could, I would make 99% of this book about mindset. It's that important. But my editor wouldn't let me. "Krista, you just wrote a book all about mindset. Just tell them to read that one." She's right.

My latest book, *Stop, Snap & Switch: Train Your Brain to Unleash Your Limitless Life*, is all about the brain hacks that helped me succeed over the years that I teach my students today. It goes step-by-step about how to work with your brain and all the research that supports it. I *strongly* urge you to read this book (it's also available in audio). It will help you literally rewire your brain, and it's as important or even more important than anything else I can share with you. I can teach you every fancy strategy and foolproof technique in the world to build your Million Dollar Month coaching or high ticket offer business, but the truth is *you just won't follow through* if you don't believe in yourself and believe that the process will work for you.

A great mindset isn't something you're born with. But you can train yourself to have it. That's great news because it means if you're starting with a crappy mindset—lots of self-doubt, fear, and pessimism—you can train yourself into a success-oriented mindset of optimism, confidence, and courage. I was at a Tony Robbins gathering recently with people who had built $350M and even billion-dollar businesses. And at least half of them had mindset issues! They said things like, "When will I feel worthy?" or "I don't feel like I'm deserving or that I'm enough." Everyone, even multi-millionaires, has issues. If they have issues, well, it's okay if you do too. We are all human, and these are things we can work on. You've got to train yourself to be super solid in this. If you aren't, you'll pull back at every little hiccup. You'll freak out at every obstacle and make rotten decisions. You'll give up when the success you want is just around the corner.

To create the coaching or high ticket offer business you want, you need to focus on having the right mindset for yourself *first*. Then, when you're coaching clients and students, you'll need to focus on helping them with *their* mindset. **No matter what you're teaching them, they need that belief in themselves and belief in what they do so they can be successful at it.** Yes, I know that you have killer techniques and strategies to teach your students. But to get them the success they're after, your training needs to incorporate *at least 50% in mindset training.* I'm telling you this from experience. Again, I urge you to read or listen to *Stop, Snap & Switch: Train Your Brain to Unleash Your Limitless Life* to get some grounding in mindset. I'm also going to give you a few Million Dollar Month Mindset exercises and tips throughout this book. For now, let's talk about three specific pieces of mindset you'll need to succeed in building a Million Dollar a Month business: *belief in yourself, belief in your product,* and *belief in ethical persuasion.*

When I talk about belief, I mean that you know something is *true beyond a shadow of a doubt.* It's as solid as knowing the sun will come up in the morning or that water is wet. You never question it. You have massive *conviction* that it is true, and because you have that conviction, you're able to demonstrate it and express it. As I always tell my students, **"He who has the most conviction wins the debate."**

Harnessing Self-Belief for Monumental Success

Okay, so what do you *really* believe about yourself? As you're reading this book, are you thinking, *Okay, well, I've lucked out so far, but maybe that's all I'm capable of?* Or maybe it's, *I'm ready to go for it!* but in the back of your mind, you're thinking about all the times you failed. It's not just you. I'd guess that J. Lo stands backstage wondering if her voice will be good that night and if she looks all right. (Can't you just picture her checking out her bootylicious in the mirror?) Winning athletes like Lionel Messi and Michael Jordan work with sports psychologists *constantly* to make sure their self-beliefs are strong. Tony Robbins, who is a master of mindset, has a full routine where he pumps himself up and reminds himself of what he's about *every single time* he speaks.

You would think that these people have all the self-confidence in the world. Yet as successful as they are, the J. Los, Tony Robbins, Lionel Messis, and Michael Jordans of the world are human too. They know that believing in yourself is not just a "one and done" exercise. It needs to be reinforced constantly. Even if you have a strong belief in yourself, it needs constant feeding. And if it's not so strong, it especially needs daily workouts to get stronger. You don't just take a shower once and figure you'll be clean forever, right? I've been working with my self-confidence for decades, and I'm still constantly working on it.

The people I'm coaching in the Million Dollar Month Model are already highly successful businesspeople, so you would think they have plenty of self-confidence. Not necessarily so. One of the people I'm coaching in MDMM is an awesome guy and probably one of the most macho-type guys that you can imagine on the internet, and he has millions and millions of followers. But as we worked together, Mr. Macho just kept saying, "I don't understand why anybody would want to be in a high ticket mastermind with me. I don't understand the value that they would get." He just couldn't get it. And I said, "Listen, the whole reason I'm as successful as I am today is because I joined a mastermind." Then I asked the other people in the room, "How many of you are in a mastermind?" About 70% of the room raised their hands. Then, I asked them what they got out of their masterminds. All said roughly the same thing. They got a few trainings. They got to meet twice a year with the head of the mastermind. And they had a vacation once a year with the group (they actually had to pay for the vacation itself), where everyone showed up to do more masterminding together. They talked about how much they got out of just being around the other people and brainstorming and masterminding with each other. They all said that alone was worth the cost of the mastermind. But Mr. Macho still couldn't get it. Then I said to everyone in the room, "How many of you would sign up if Mr. Macho had a mastermind? How many of you from this room would pay $50,000 to join it?" Five people out of 15 people raised their hands. So literally one-third of the room raised their hands and said they'd pay $50k to join him. After that, I had another meeting with him and said, "So, do you see it now?" And you know what he said?

"Well, I'm still not sure."

I'm thinking, *Oh my gosh. What more evidence do you want?!?*

Another student in my Million Dollar Month Model group teaches women how to feel confident with money and spending money to grow their businesses. Yet, I could see that she herself was not confident about spending money. I said to her, "Look, you don't get what you want. You get what you are. You're preaching about feeling comfortable spending money so you can make more, yet you're afraid to spend money on marketing your own program." She said, "I just don't have the belief. I'm just not sure I can make it work." So, I coached her back up, talked her off the ledge, and one week later, she invested the money she needed to invest in marketing—and she crushed it! You would've thought that these highly successful people would've been different and more confident than other people, but they were the same.

Self-confidence does *not* mean that you believe you're perfect. In fact, for many reasons, as a coach, it's better if you know that you are *not* perfect and share it with your students (I'll explain more about this in later chapters). You aren't perfect, but self-confidence means that you know *for sure* that you are strong enough and smart enough to do what you want to do. You know *for certain* that you are resourceful and can figure out how to get through, over, or around any obstacles. You know with *true conviction* that you *can* do this, and you *will* do this, that you won't let the naysayers hold you back.

When you aren't 100% confident, when you let those tiny irritating self-doubts float around in your head, you simply won't put your whole self into whatever you're trying to do. You'll put your toe in the water, but you won't jump in. Now you might be saying, "But Krista, I'm pretty sure I can do this." "Pretty sure" is not enough. (And it won't be enough for your students.) "Pretty sure" will let you back out when the going gets tough or an unexpected disappointment hits you in the face. BTW, you should *expect* this to happen. Failure goes hand in hand with greatness. Amazing things don't typically come easily. And with "pretty sure," you'll end up folding when it gets difficult. You'll keep doing the easy things, meaningless busy work, to avoid the important, scarier tasks that will really make a difference.

Instead of "pretty sure," you need to be able to say to yourself, "I will never give up until I have built the business I want! I am unstoppable!" You'll have to know "I'm doing this, no matter what. There is no alternative!" Of course, being human, every once in a while, a nasty doubt will sneak in. What do you do then? You kick it to the curb! (*Stop, Snap & Switch: Train Your Brain to Unleash Your Limitless Life* will show you how to do that.)

Equipping Your Students With Unshakeable Self-Belief

Your students are coming to you for a reason. Let's say your program teaches people how to build highly successful professional businesses. An accountant is taught to be an accountant, or an insurance agent is taught to be an insurance agent. Lawyers and dentists go through years of extra schooling to learn their profession. They're all taught specific skills, but they're not usually taught how to run a business and make the money they want to make. Or say you're coaching married couples or parents. Couples are taught how to tie the knot but not how to make the marriage really work for them. Parents know how to make a baby, but they aren't given a manual on how to raise a good, happy kid. So, they *do* come to you for *information* because (hopefully) you've been there and done that. You've made some mistakes. You've learned what not to do and what to do along the way. You can help them, so they don't have to make the same mistakes you made. You can show them the winning tactics and strategies you've created or picked up along the way.

But if all they needed was information, they could find it in a million places. They could just do a Google search and have all the information they need at their fingertips. If they want to lose weight, or eat healthy food, or start their own pizza parlor, all the information they could ever want is immediately available on their laptop. But the thing is that information alone won't get them where they want to go. You may be offering them cutting-edge information that is not widely available. But your amazing information alone can't give them the success they want. *The reason that they aren't where they want to be is not for a lack of information. It's that they have a limiting mindset.* They lack belief in themselves, and they lack belief that anything will work for them. And *that's* why they need you. They are missing the *who* in the equation. You can "how to" yourself to death, but the *who* (you) is the key to them being able to put it all together.

When I first started my real estate coaching, I wanted to give them all the tactics and strategies I'd figured out over the years that helped me sell 100 homes a year every year. "Here's the listing presentation. Here are the funnels. Here's the CRM. Here's all the stuff that you need." People were doing okay, but I was surprised that they weren't moving faster.

Then, I started doing a free training that was really mindset-driven. I threw in a couple of small tactics and helped people get small wins but then really focused on the mindset that they would need to succeed. I started noticing that this mindset group with the free training was getting more success faster than my paid coaching students, who had been given tons of strategies! "What? What's going on here?" The difference was that I had skipped all the mindset stuff for my students when I first started out. I thought that they wanted the tactics, and they did. But what I didn't realize was that, even though I gave them awesome tactics, if their mindset isn't right, the tactics won't matter.

I had to redo the entire first three weeks of my program (and when I developed my MDMM course, I made sure mindset was a *huge* focus of the trainings). I focused on their mindset, and the results were so much better! I realized that I had to continue to work with their mindsets over and over and over again. I had to keep on bringing it up. Why? These people had spent decades living with mindsets that were negative and sabotaging them. It's like going to the gym. One workout is not going to whip that flab into six-pack abs. It has to be consistent. Or it's like going to church. You don't just show up at church one Sunday and find God. You go to church more often than that to strengthen and maintain your relationship with God.

A good coach is constantly teaching people and getting people to believe in themselves. A great coach has such conviction and belief that their students are able to borrow that belief until they have built up their own. As a coach, I tell my students, "Hey, if you don't believe in yourself, borrow my belief because I believe. I know this can work. I believe in you. I know you are hardworking, and you deserve this. I know this can work for you because I've seen it happen so many times. While you're working on believing more in yourself, use my belief in you to get you through."

I have to keep on weaving mindset teaching into my trainings every single week. That's when my students have the most success. Everything in terms of tactics and strategies that they need, whether it's in real estate or in building a Million Dollar Month Model coaching/high ticket offer business, is inside my program. I sometimes feel like, "Oh, I need to give them more strategies and tactics. Something different, something new." Everything they really need is already there. Even if I never taught any new strategies, it wouldn't make a difference. They have all the tools they need to be successful. (Please don't get me wrong. We update the programs monthly to be current and based on what we learn from optimizing and testing). But even with all that great information, *I still have to work on their mindset every single week.*

You'll have to do it constantly to get people to believe in themselves, literally on a weekly, daily basis, because people lose that belief so easily. They get all excited and see that others just like them have succeeded. Then—wham!—some well-meaning (or just plain mean) person tells them that they shouldn't get their hopes up. Someone reminds them of all the times they failed or talks about other people who failed. Some Negative Nellie throws cold water on their vision for themselves. Honestly, it doesn't take much to send people into a tailspin. Something happens during their day. They get a mean email, or someone is rude to them, and they spiral down. It's like a popsicle sitting out in the sun on a hot summer day. It starts out solid, but in less than a minute, it turns into a sticky, gooey mess!

That's why you'll need to constantly transfer your positive energy onto people so they will succeed. Your goal is not just to hand them the tools and processes and say, "Okay, my job is done." No! You want them to succeed! Your success is dependent on their success. And for them to succeed, you *have* to keep them being inspired, and being motivated, and being engaged. You have to keep them believing in themselves.

Your people will face discouragement. Things always take longer than people want. Everyone comes up against roadblocks when they are trying to change. They'll step out of their comfort zone and freak out. If they're working on their business, it will affect their personal life. If they're working on their relationship, it will ooze over into their work life. Your job is to help them maneuver and weave through the roadblocks in all areas of life.

When I survey my real estate students about "What's the most impactful part of the Mashore Model program?" at least 95% of them say "mindset." Yes, the strategies and techniques I taught them made a huge difference to their businesses. But ***the reason they were able to follow through and do what they needed to do was that they built a stronger belief in themselves.*** They learned to feel positive more naturally and more often rather than feeling negative. I cannot stress enough how important mindset training is to your students' success—and, therefore, to yours.

The Power of Product Confidence

Another specific belief you need to have is a rock-solid belief in your program or product. Hopefully, you're not trying to teach something that you just *know* about, but you're teaching something that you've actually experienced and used in your own life to succeed. Whether you're teaching some aspect of your profession or whether you've been through a tough situation (like divorce, eating disorder, loss of a career, loss of a child, etc.) even if you haven't yet officially coached anyone, hopefully you've mentored someone who has used what you teach, and it helped them succeed or get through that same difficult circumstance.

You need to have conviction that what you're teaching or offering can work for *anyone* if they work it. It can be replicated, and they don't need some Superhero level of talent and courage or an Einstein level of genius to work for them. Yes, they'll have to apply what you're teaching, and some of your students might have to work harder at it than others. But you have to have the conviction that, if they stick with it, they *will* succeed. It's your conviction that will help them believe in themselves.

You also need to know with *certainty* in your gut that the benefits your clients will receive from your product far outweigh whatever they'll be paying for it. They aren't just throwing money away, but they are *investing* in their future happiness and success. You're giving more than you're getting (which, by the way, is a basic success principle in any kind of business or relationship).

As I'm writing this, my real estate program is priced at $23,997, and I know for certain that they can make that back and more within six months by following what I teach them. I also know that they'll be happier in all the other areas of their lives. Some of my students have seen results within a few weeks. Others have taken months to really see results. It all depends on the person, how committed they are and the time, marketing money, and energy they invest into it. Sooner or later, I know if they work my program and stick with it, it will work for them.

The biggest mistake I see people making is giving up too early and not giving the process the time it takes to work. A lot of successful people will tell you that this is the biggest downfall for most people. They don't give it the time it takes to succeed. They stop when they are, as Napoleon Hill would say, "Three feet from gold." Part of your job is to help them stay the course and not give up because they believe so completely that what you offer will make them more successful.

In some programs, value and benefits can't be calculated in terms of money. So, how do you compare the price of your offering with the value they will receive? For example, your program might be about having a great marriage. In that case, the value is the difference between spending the next twenty years in a painful marriage (or getting divorced) versus having an awesome, supportive, fulfilling marriage. Or maybe your program focuses on health and wellness. If your program really delivers and improves people's health, the benefits are priceless, right? To help you have the conviction you need for products like this that aren't tied to financial success, find a way to measure the results (we'll talk about this more in Chapter 5). You can have them take surveys before and after in that area of their life. One good way to measure is to have them write down the specific outcomes they want (i.e., "I want to have more romantic evenings with my spouse" or "I want my kids to feel safe talking to me about their problems"). Then, have them keep track of the positive steps they have toward each outcome and also when they finally achieve the outcomes they want.

What if you don't have a rock-solid belief in your program? You can do a couple of things. You can take some students under your wing for free, run them through the program, and help them get results. If you're missing anything or need to add extra value and training, your freebie group will help you understand what you need to tweak. Seeing this group succeed will also give you confidence that what you're teaching in the program really works. (Plus, it will give you some testimonials to use as social proof once you're ready to launch your program.) Why is believing in your product so important? Because if you don't have 100% conviction that your product works, your clients won't either.

If you know your program works but still don't have 100% conviction about it, I'm guessing it's a self-belief issue. You might be thinking, *Well, yeah, it works, but who am I to teach it? I know the material, but why would they listen to me?* If you hear yourself saying things like that, it's your belief in yourself, not your program, that needs work.

Getting Your Students to Believe in Your Product

Have you ever read those placebo studies? They give half of the group some kind of medication, and the other half gets a sugar pill with no medication in it at all. The patients don't know who got sugar pills and who got the real medicine. The researchers tell all of them in both groups that this medication is absolutely guaranteed to work. And you know what? In many cases, the sugar pill is just about as effective as the drug. That's the power of belief.

People react differently if they are convinced something is going to work. If they aren't certain because you aren't certain, they tend to "try it out" without fully buying in. This makes a huge difference in the results they get. So, one of your main jobs, starting with your promotional events and continuing throughout your entire program, is to make sure people completely believe that this will work for them if they apply themselves. They need to drink the Kool-Aid. I don't mean this in a manipulative way. You aren't trying to get them to believe in something that isn't true. You're helping them have the faith that you have that it absolutely will work for them.

Depending on what you're teaching or offering them, they may need to learn to have absolute conviction about their own product or vehicle as well. If a dentist isn't sure that her services are excellent, will she be able to build a business? If an entrepreneur doesn't believe that his product is truly valuable, he'll never succeed, no matter what marketing software you give him. So, as you're working to build their belief in you and your vehicle, help them also gain more belief in their own offering.

If you can get the people that you want to coach to believe in themselves and in you and your product, you're halfway there. They need to believe in the *vehicle*, which is what you're selling. For my real estate coaching business, the vehicle is video and social media and becoming a master marketer. If I can get them to believe in the vehicle and in me and then work on their internal and external beliefs, I can help them. Building belief in your vehicle is a big part of the entire MDMM program, as you'll see in future chapters. The process starts when you get someone to first raise their hand agreeing with something you say and goes all the way through to conversion. Belief in themselves plus belief in me and my product is the winning combination.

One last specific piece of mindset that you need to build your MDMM high ticket offer or coaching business is…

Ethical Persuasion

In sales, they used to talk about being so good that you could sell ice to an Eskimo. What I don't like about that is that it sounds like you're selling something that the customer doesn't really need or want! To me, that's not ethical. It's self-serving, and that's not what I'm about. I'm about service and giving true value, not just making the sale. But because I have *total conviction* that my product will really serve them and improve their lives, I am great at sales. I have no hesitation about pulling out all the stops to help them say "yes."

When you stop thinking of selling as yucky, you'll sell more. I strongly believe that *sales is service*. I know I am providing value, and I also know that, without my help, it will take them years and years and millions of dollars in trial and error to learn what I know I can give them. If they follow my model, they'll start getting the results they're looking for in *months* as compared to years. But If I didn't feel this way, if I didn't know this with absolute certainty, I couldn't sell the way I do.

If you cringe a little bit at the idea of using sales techniques to get potential students to say "yes," you aren't alone. I did an exclusive workshop a while back teaching several massively successful people my Million Dollar Month Model. These people had already built incredible businesses, so you know that they had to be involved in sales, right? Yet when we got to this part of the workshop, some of them had hesitation. Their doubts usually showed up in questions like, "What if they can't afford it?" "What if my list isn't big enough?" "What if I'm not a great presenter?"

So, in that workshop, I shared the story of a student of mine, Lisa Graham, who attended one of my events several years ago. Back then, my coaching program was $10,000. Lisa was broke, in an abusive relationship, and struggling with her real estate business. She actually drained her savings account to join the program in the Spring of 2018. In 2018, she increased production by $4.3 million. In 2019, it dropped to $1.9 million as she went through her divorce and focused on her son who was struggling. In 2020, she was back up to $4.4 million, increased it to $8.8 million in 2021, and grew to $10 million in 2022.

When your mindset is right, you are able to create and receive. When it's not right, you are striving and anxious, and you drag through the day. The right mindset gives you energy and focus. Yes, Lisa learned a ton of great techniques and strategies from me. But she couldn't have done what she did if I hadn't helped her with her mindset. And I'm happy to report Lisa is getting married in a few weeks and looks happier than ever. And all of this happened because I helped her say "yes" to herself using ethical persuasion. That's what you are trying to get people to do. I was helping Lisa financially with a business opportunity, but with the mindset training and all that goes along with it, she became a new woman and created a new life. That's why we do what we do. Think about it: What if I hadn't had the confidence and used the tools to persuade Lisa to join my program? Can you imagine how her life would be different right now? That's ethical persuasion. My job is to get Lisa to say "yes" to herself. And that's your job, too. She could not have done it on her own.

I've had students tap their 401(k)s, sell their cars, and max out their credit cards. Do I feel guilty about that? No! Because I know that my program will more than make up for it. They'll make that money back and more. They'll be happier in their careers. Their personal lives will improve. I've seen it over and over.

Here's the point: If I have conviction that my program will truly serve them and make their lives better, I am doing them a *disservice* by not doing everything I can to ethically persuade them to sign up. Of course, I would never *force* anyone to join, even if I could. No one wants to be *convinced*. But people do want you to *help persuade* them to do what they really want to do when they can't convince themselves to do it on their own. That's a service! If I let my own fears and lack of self-confidence get in the way of persuading them to their better life, shame on me. Shame on me for taking away the good stuff that could be theirs.

I've got an amazing sales team (I'll talk about them more later). They know that the old way of "pressure sales" (intimidating someone until they sign on the dotted line) is no good. You do *not* want people in your program who really don't want to be there! That said, many potential students are a little hesitant. That's natural because it's a lot of money and a big investment. Yet if we can find an ethical way to persuade them, get through their fears, and help them believe they can succeed with us, it's our responsibility to do that.

I want you to embrace ethical persuasion. (Depending on the type of clients you're training or product you offer, you may need to help *them* embrace ethical persuasion for their businesses as well.) We aren't selling ice to Eskimos. We're offering people a lifeline. A way to get what they really want out of life. A chance to be the person they've always wanted to be. Do *not* take that away from them just because you have some limiting beliefs about sales!

Many of the components of the Million Dollar Month Model are based on ethical persuasion. It begins in the very beginning of the sales funnel (more on this in Chapter 8) when you're simply giving them great information and insight for free. I use ethical persuasion all through the events, and we've gotten it down to a science. Some of the ethical persuasion I use comes from the psychological approach that NLP (neuro-linguistic programming) uses and a lot of other strategies that I'll explain in later chapters.

Yes, there are specific techniques, but, no, it isn't about manipulation. Think of it this way: If someone speaks a different language than you do, will they understand you better if you speak in their language? If someone was racing down a path that is a dead end, wouldn't you do them a service by showing them another route? To me, manipulation is when you try to get someone to do what you want them to do that *isn't* in their best interest. Using the techniques I use, I'm persuading people to do what *is* in their best interest, something they really want to do but are feeling afraid or hesitant. Is it also what I want them to do? Heck, yeah! Because I know it will help them get the success they want.

The Elephants in the Room

Based on my own experience and now the experience of my MDMM students, I know for sure that you have some specific fears and limiting beliefs about your ability to succeed at the Million Dollar Month Model. We've all had them, so let's tackle them up front:

But I don't have a big enough list! How will I ever fill my events?

I'm telling you that this is one area where size does *not* matter! Especially in the beginning, you just need enough contacts to get started. I'll be showing you other ways to get people to attend your events in Chapters 2 and 8, but you can begin with what you've got and build on it. Tim, one of my students who certifies people in a particular type of hypnosis he created, started with a tiny list and pretty much nothing for an advertising budget. At his first 3-day event, he only had 30 people (which is about how many I had years ago for my first event). Out of those 30, he enrolled 6 for a total of $103,000! Not bad for a tiny list. Another student, Tiffany, who teaches marketing strategies for mortgage officers had fewer than 57 people by the time she made her offer during the 3-day event. Of those, eight people signed up, which brought in $143,976. (By the way, I'll give you real examples of my students in this book, though some of the names have been changed to protect privacy.)

But I'm not a good public speaker!

While I love to teach, I *definitely* did not love public speaking. Being in front of groups terrified me. I remember that early in my career in real estate, just being on tours with other Realtors®, where I had to talk about my listings, made my knees shake. I was so nervous once that I said my own name wrong! I called myself Krista Miller (my ex-husband's last name) when I had gone back to Krista Vitale (my maiden name). Obviously, the public speaking part of building my coaching business did *not* come naturally to me.

Over the years, I've gotten training and have really worked at it. But I didn't have all that going when I started my real estate coaching business. It was more like on-the-job training. It wasn't easy. What I did have, though, even from the beginning, was a burning desire to coach people and help them achieve the success they wanted. That desire kept me going, even when I stumbled over words or forgot what I was saying in the middle of a webinar.

My student Tiffany had never taught in front of a group before her first webinar, and she was really nervous about it. "When it was over, I looked over at my husband who was listening in and helping me admit people into the Zoom room. He turned to me, looking surprised, and said, 'You did so well!' And I felt like I did. When the camera turned on, something came out of me that I didn't know was there. I was able to be funny and witty, and it became so fun. I was still nervous for the 3-day event, but I felt like I brought so much energy. I was on fire."

My people can't afford it! My people don't have the time!

Let me ask you something: If you were really sick and the only treatment that could completely heal you cost you six months of your income and hours of treatments, would you go for it? Would you think it was worth it? If you were deeply in love with your spouse but having trouble in your marriage, would you pay thousands of dollars to someone who you knew had the skills to bring you back together? Would you invest whatever time it took to save your marriage?

In the beginning, most of my students have said something like, "My people won't/can't pay that kind of money." One of my MDMM students, Enrique, lives in Madrid. His potential clients live in Spain (where the median monthly income is $1500) and throughout Latin America (where the median monthly income is about $500). Based on that market, he had a hard time believing that he could price his offer at $16,000. But he followed the system and did it. His first 3-day event, he had about 500 people, and 240 of them booked calls with his salespeople. "Many people, like 70% of them, were not so much qualified, but 30% of them were. We closed 27 sales, which for the first time is fantastic. So, we have broken the belief that this would be impossible to do."

Yes, it's true that not everyone has the money to invest in a high ticket offer, and some people really do have limited time. But you aren't looking for everyone. You're looking for people who are really motivated to get the results your program or offer can give them.

No one knows me. Who would listen to me?

Maybe no one knows you yet, but I'll show you how you can become known. I'll also show you how to become an authority through video and engagement marketing (Chapter 8). When I first started coaching, no one outside of my local community knew me either. I had done a good job of marketing myself and my brand as a great agent, but no one associated me with being a coach. It didn't come overnight, but I just started with what I had. I created content and did videos. I did paid ads and started presenting to different real estate groups. I coached some people for free to get testimonials. I even wrote my first book! I did everything I could think of to get my name out there as a coach. But I didn't wait until I was well-known to start putting my coaching business together. I just jumped in.

Finding Your Why: Unraveling Your Deep-Rooted Motivation

Honestly, one of the best ways to get through the limiting beliefs I just mentioned or any fears you might have is to find your compelling *why*. Getting in touch with the real reason you want to build your MDMM business will give you the energy and motivation to blast through any doubts and keep moving forward. Just "making more money" is not what I mean by a compelling why, and it won't really cut it when you're building your MDMM business. Your why has to be deeper than that. It can be a carrot (something you want), a stick (something that you really don't want), or both. But it has to be something that is so compelling that you won't let anything get in your way.

For example, my first real estate business (before I got into coaching) was mainly built out of *desperation* (a stick), which is a super strong motivation and a very compelling why. This started in 2003 on a Saturday morning. I was at breakfast with five of my girlfriends and all our kids. We had all gone to high school together, and our children were growing up together. It was a perfect Saturday morning, laughing, reminiscing, kids running around playing. My phone rang, and it was a friend of mine from college. She told me she had just seen my husband in Napa. I said, "Oh yes. He's there at a golf thing for work." She said, "No, Krista, I'm so sorry, but I saw him being intimate with another woman."

My heart started pounding; my face got hot and flushed; my eyes instantly teared up. I felt like I'd been punched in the stomach with hurt and anger. My mind started racing in a crazy loop: *But we have kids. We built this life together. How many more lies did he tell? How could he be so foolish to throw this all away?"* Even worse, this was not the first time something like this had happened. I felt humiliated and angry at myself for "allowing" it to happen again.

19

I drove home, doing my best to hold back the tears so that my daughters couldn't see. And before I could even really wrap my mind around what was going on, I *knew* I was going to have to save myself. More importantly, I knew I was going to have to take care of my daughters and give them the life they deserved. I didn't know what that was going to look like or how I was going to do that. I had just left my safe, secure, full-time job as a 3rd grade teacher to get into real estate. My plan was to work a less hectic, structured schedule so I could spend more time at home with my daughters. But now, that plan just flew out the window. I didn't have a Plan B and had no idea what to do next. But I remember a little voice inside saying, "You know, Krista, your world is about to change drastically, and you need to be ready for it."

In an instant, my whole world turned upside down. I panicked, thinking I might lose my daughters, or they might not be able to live with me. I was freaked thinking my kids could lose their home, that they'd lose any sense of normalcy being thrown back and forth between their father and me. My life got so crazy. Within a week of my husband leaving me and tearing up what I thought was our happy home (I guess we all think that our world is fine before it's torn apart!), I watched my two daughters being picked up by the new girlfriend who was driving *my* car! My bank accounts were completely drained, and we had just bought a new home. I mean, who can even make up such a mess? Well, in a matter of days, this was my life.

Statistically, divorce is pretty common. Everyone seems to get divorced. It's normal, right? But it isn't normal for me, and it isn't normal in my family. My parents have been married for over 55 years, and my brothers for 25 and 30 years. I think that made it even more devastating to me.

Yet in the midst of it all, I knew I needed to be able to support myself and my girls and give us a real life. It was up to me.

That realization propelled me to become the rookie of the year in my first year in real estate. It got me to work smart and hard, selling 69 homes my first year and averaging at least 135 homes every single year thereafter. It was the motivation, the why, that built my business and put me in the top 1% of all Realtors® in the nation. Not because I wanted to. I'd been thrown into survival mode. I'm the person who had not lived at home since I was 13 and was displaced from my family. That made my *why* (keeping my kids happy and safe in our home) incredibly strong and the driving force to my success.

That was the big, ugly stick that pushed me to do more than I ever thought I could. The carrot part was wanting to build a really positive environment for my daughters to grow up in. I had not lived at home since I was 13, so I felt I had missed out on something, and I didn't want them to miss out. The morning that the new girlfriend came and picked up my daughters, driving my car, I sat in my kitchen drinking wine early in the morning (Don't judge me! It was a rough morning!) and staring at the backyard. We had just bought the home and moved in a few months before my husband and I split up, so we hadn't even landscaped the back. It was just dirt. I wanted to put flowers in the back. I wanted to build a playground and put in a pool so they could have their buddies over. I wanted that backyard to become a place where we could create great family memories. Even though I had that desire, I have to admit that the stick was probably stronger than the carrot at this time. Desperation can make people do all kinds of amazing things.

When I started my first coaching business, it was out of passion, not desperation. Back then, I was doing really well in real estate, and I became passionate about helping others find the success I had found. Helping others has always been a huge part of my life, and coaching seemed like the perfect way to do that. Helping others succeed was my compelling why. Then, when I succeeded with my real estate coaching business, I realized that I could make an even greater impact if I helped other coaches expand their reach using the Million Dollar Month Model so they could help even more people. They would be able to affect the lives of people I would never run into. It's like creating a huge ripple effect. So, for both of my coaching businesses, my compelling why was to help others.

I was talking to Dean Graziosi, who was interviewing me for a speaking gig. He talked about being back to his childhood home recently, and he was with all these men who were his best friends from high school. He said, "You know, these men are no different than I am. In fact, I'm probably not as smart as most of them. They didn't take the risk and so they're stuck at their jobs, and they don't feel any fulfillment. They're just waiting to retire. But me? I love what I do, and I've been able to make an impact." He started talking about the Ideal Client (they call her Julie) for one of their programs. "There are so many Julies out there who are stuck and who need our help. We need to show them a way that they can have everything and that it's not too late and that they deserve it all." And I could feel how passionate and sincere he was about it. Yes, he has personal whys for building his business. But being passionate about serving others and helping Julie is definitely one of the reasons he is so successful.

Whatever Your Vehicle, You Need to Train Mindset

Are you convinced that you need to do mindset training with your students so they will succeed? And that you need to improve your own mindset for you to succeed as an MDMM coach or while crafting your high ticket offer. You may not have even thought much about mindset before, and now I'm telling you that you need to become great at teaching it! As I mentioned in the introduction, at least 50% of your training and virtual events needs to be in mindset if you want your clients to succeed.

I've always been a personal growth junkie, and I've trained with some of the best. I started early on because of a tough childhood that left me with plenty of self-doubt and negative beliefs. I'm still always looking for books and seminars to learn more about the brain and how to get it to work for you (not against you). So, for me, when I realized that I needed to incorporate it into my training, it was easy. I had a lot of material and experience to draw from.

You may have to do some groundwork in this area. To get a good foundation, start with *Stop, Snap & Switch: Train Your Brain to Unleash Your Limitless Life* (also available in audio). Pay attention to the short Million Dollar Month Mindset exercises in this book. I've listed some of my favorite books and authors at Theprovenmodel.com/resources. Yes, it might take you some effort to learn what you need to learn, but it will be totally worth it for the success of your business and your students' success!

Scan this QR code using the camera app on your phone to access your resource page & added freebies now!

MDMM Mindset: Finding Your Why

I use the Seven Levels of Why that I learned from Dean Graziosi (who learned it from someone else). I'm honestly not sure why it's seven layers, but whenever I use it myself or coach someone else to use it, seven seems to be the right number. Take out a piece of paper and write down "Question #1: Why is building a Million Dollar Month business important to you?" Write down your answer. For example, maybe your answer to Question #1 is "Because I want to expand my business." Question # 2 is, "Why is expanding your business so important to you?" Maybe your answer is, "Because I want to make more money." Okay, so take that answer into Question #3 so it reads, "Why is making more money so important to you?" Maybe you respond that you want to send your children to college. Question #4 then would be, "Why is sending your children to college so important to you?" Get the picture? Keep asking and answering until you end up with a reason why that makes you emotional. It's no longer just an idea of something that would be nice to have. You should start to feel really excited and inspired about having it, or maybe you really feel the painful cost of *not* having it.

Once you find your why, write it down. Keep it in front of you so that when you get off-track or discouraged, you remember why you can't give up!

CHAPTER 2

7 Levers for 7 Figures

This chapter will give you an overview of the entire client acquisition and conversion framework that makes up the Million Dollar Month Model by showing you all the things we track each month. Honestly, I owe a lot of my success to the fact that we *track, test, and optimize everything* we do and the results we are getting. We tweak and change one thing each event to see how it will affect our event, revenue, success, etc. That's the only way to tell if everything you're doing is getting the results you want. If something is getting terrific results, great! Do more of it! If it isn't, then it's time to tweak it or even drop it altogether. It's crazy to keep doing the same thing over and over if it isn't getting you what you want, right?

Tracking results applies to everything from the ads you run to the bonus gifts you give to the order that you present your content. Literally, we track everything I'll show you in this book. Every piece of what you're doing has to be effective. And you don't just track something one time and call it good. You have to keep tracking. Trends change because of all kinds of different factors (the economy, the news, even the weather!), so what worked before may not be working now. Tracking needs to be incorporated into everything you do, and you need to check your results frequently.

One reason that the Million Dollar Month Model 3-day virtual event has gotten such amazing results is that we track the heck out of every little aspect of it. That's how we came up with the winning MDMM formula, the pieces of the puzzle, and the order they go in. And as we've tracked these events over the years, we've realized that there are 7 key things that have to be on target for the event to succeed. I now teach them as the 7 Levers for 7 Figures. Think about the levers that let water through canal systems. If the levers are all the way open, the water flows freely. But if the levers are only partially open or there's a lever that's hardly open at all, the water won't flow. Each lever is important. If one isn't working, the water will get backed up somewhere. And by the time you get to the end, you'll have just a trickle, not the flood you want!

Lever # 1: Registrations

Registrations are coming from your free webinars as well as from the additional marketing you do for the virtual event itself. If you've just got a trickle of registrations coming through this lever, you're toast! I'll teach you how to use the Money to Math calculator in Chapter 8. Basically, you figure out how many people you need to sign up for your program, then backtrack and, using your conversion rate, figure out how many people you need to attend your virtual event. Then do everything you can to get them there! You'll get better as you practice, but you might assume a 5% conversion at first. It's very conservative, but there are tons of variables, including the effectiveness of your sales team.

I talk about marketing in general in Chapter 8 and here are some of the specific ways we market our webinar and our MDMM 3-day virtual event:

We do paid ads and organic postings on Facebook, Instagram, YouTube, Google Ads, and TikTok. We add comments on our pages and in Facebook groups telling people to direct message (DM) us through Facebook Messenger if they want a valuable piece of content. When they DM us, we give them the piece we offered, and now we continue to develop a relationship with them. Then we invite them to the event. Once they register and show up for the event, we keep engaging with them using DM during the event by asking questions like how they like the training and whether they need anything or have any questions. The leads we bring in through messenger and have DM conversations with are higher quality, show up more, and convert at a higher rate. So, this process not only helps with registrations, it also helps with show rate, stay rate, and conversion rate.

I market the virtual event on my podcasts by giving them some teasers of what I'll be teaching. I also talk about it when I'm a guest on other people's podcasts or in their trainings and Facebook groups. We have some strategic partners whose audience or students are within my target market, so they would be likely candidates for my program. So, I'll do specific high-value trainings for those partners to gain access to their people. After the training, I invite the audience to my next event, whether it's a webinar or a 3-day virtual event. All roads eventually lead to our 3-day virtual event.

We've tested a bunch of different aspects of registration to make sure this lever is strong. For example, we discovered that people who paid to register were higher-quality leads and were more likely to show up to the event. We found that those who didn't pay were lower-quality leads who had a lower rate of showing up to the event. This isn't surprising. People tend to value something they've paid for more than a freebie. Also, those who pay are usually more likely to become high-ticket clients and invest in our coaching program than those with free tickets.

Then we tested the event ticket price and tried different pricing—$27, $47, $67, and $97. When we compared $47 versus $97, we discovered that there was little to no difference at all in lead quality and just a slight difference in show up rate. Most importantly, conversions to my $24k offer were also about the same. So, should we have kept it at $97 to get that extra $50? No! The lower price *did* increase ticket sales, which means we had more people attending, and we were able to build our list, continue to nurture these people, add more value, and make more offers to them. The CPA (cost per acquisition) or CPL (cost per lead) significantly decreased when we charged $47.00 because when we charged less, we got more people. The good news was that the quality of leads and conversions did not go down. They were basically the same. The $47 ticket price meant that this lever was wide open, and we were getting the people we needed to register, stay, and enroll in our program. This more affordable price didn't affect conversions.

Lever #2: Show Up Rate

You might be the kind of person who always shows up because you said you would so you might not understand why people flake out after they've registered. Trust me, it's really common. Life gets in the way, or people get distracted and forget. We've learned that putting tons of effort into getting them to *show up* is necessary and totally worth it. We do this from two directions: engagement and reminders.

For the engagement piece, we want to build a connection to me and my brand. So, we send out a gift that includes one of my books and our Stop, Snap and Switch bracelet. These are things they can (and do) actually use, not just throw-away pens or refrigerator magnets. Giving a gift sets up the law of reciprocity. Because they were given something valuable, they feel more responsible about showing up. We're also demonstrating that we go the extra mile for them, which helps elevate the value of our program in their eyes. Also, if they don't convert, the book and bracelet will continue to remind them of me. Within the book, we include a 5x7 marketing card that directs them to their event dashboard. It also redirects them back to the Landing Page where we offer the 3-day event. Many people go to the 3-day event 2-3 times before they enroll. So, we want to keep reminding them to go back.

We've also done other gifts: cups that say *"Community Market Leader"* (I want them to identify with becoming that), a copy of our manifesto, sticks with colorful cardboard circles they can hold up during the event that says *"$75k"* or *"Do It Now!"* We've sent sticker books and coloring books to keep the kids occupied during the three days (my Ideal Client often has young ones at home). I've also given them coupons to bribe the kids and spouse: *"Here is a coupon for an hour foot rub if you help with the kids so I can focus"* or *"2 scoops of ice cream if you allow daddy/mommy to focus and not be distractions."* We've also done spinners, so people can spin if they get fidgety (people love those).

We also set them up immediately in the private event Facebook group. We ask them to engage with others in the group by posting a little bit about themselves and what they want to gain from the event. We might do a few quick FB Lives in the weeks leading up to the event, and my team posts event reminders and inspirational messages there.

Prior to the event, our CRM also sends engagement emails with videos, pre-work for them to do in preparation for the event, offers to "invite a friend for free, and other freebies. We also incentivize them to bring a friend by giving them a digital gift when they do. They get texts with inspirational video messages to build up their excitement. The CRM also sends them a link to the digital workbook so they can download it before the event. All of their resources are also in the event dashboard.

The event dashboard is one of our best sources of engagement. The dashboard has a bunch of resources, upsells, event materials, and event details. All of our pre-event communication urges them to log into their dashboard. Rather than assuming they'll just figure it out all on their own, we use the concierge approach and walk them through it. We set them up with a pre-event tech call to boost their confidence, show them all the resources in their dashboard, and answer any questions.

Scan this QR code using the camera app on your phone to access your resource page & added freebies now!

Our main efforts in reminders also come through our CRM, so most of it is automated. Registrants first get a confirmation email that confirms the dates and times and gives them the Zoom link, FB page link, and instructions for logging into their event dashboard. In the week before the event, we send reminder *emails* 7 days out, 5 days out, 3 days out, and the night before. We also send reminder *texts* 1 week before, 3 days before, and the night before the event. Then on each morning of the event, we send a text 30 minutes before the event starts. But we don't stop there! On Day 1, we'll send an email during the morning and after the training is over for the day. We'll send texts to everyone during the event before a section of super valuable training.

We will tell people to DM (Direct Message) me if they would like a valuable piece of content, and then when they DM us, we give them the valuable piece we promised. But now we continue to develop a relationship with them even though they've already registered. Then we keep engaging with them even during the event, asking how they like it, if they need anything, have any questions, etc. The people who we bring in through messenger and have direct messenger conversations with are higher quality, and they show up more and convert at a higher rate. So, using DM helps with registration, show rate, stay rate, and conversion rate.

A huge benefit of our dashboard is that we can identify who has engaged and who hasn't engaged prior to the event. If they haven't engaged by logging into their dashboard or showing up for their tech call by the Thursday before the event, we put them on a reminder call list. Our Virtual Assistants make the calls on Friday, Saturday, and Sunday (the event starts on Monday) to remind them and see if they need any help logging in. You'd be surprised at how many times people have missed our emails (going to spam or promo files) and texts (we have the wrong number).

We actually try to call *everyone* who registered, but the people who did not sign into their dashboard are high priority. During these calls, we make sure that they have signed into their dashboard, have their resources, and have downloaded/printed out their workbook (which are on the dashboard). We let them know how excited we are that we'll be seeing them on X date and Y time. And we've learned that by asking these two additional questions, more people show up, and conversions go up. #1: "Krista wants to know if you have any questions for her." #2: "Krista would like to know if there is anything specific you hope that she covers." This helps them know we care and lets them know that they are going to get their most important questions answered and that we definitely will be covering something that will be of interest to them.

Does this sound like overkill? Remember, if they don't attend the event, there's no way you can convert them! There's no way you can help them get what they want or help them succeed. If this lever isn't totally open, you can end up with lots of registrations but tons of no-shows. People need the extra nudge to get the help they need. The MDMM system works. Follow the system!

Lever #3: Stay Rate

Now that you've gotten them to show up, the next lever is to get them to *stay* in the event so they can hear what you have to say and learn what you have to teach them. A lot of this has to do with your presentation skills and ability to capture and keep their attention. You may not be a great presenter yet, but remember that mindset trumps skill set every time. You don't have to be perfect, but you need to be enthusiastic, energetic, and authentic to keep their attention. You'll get better with time and practice and the MDMM map to guide you. We've tested each puzzle piece and designed the map of the event to balance out mindset training with tactical and strategic training. We know that it works because we've tested it so much, so follow the map!

Doing the 3-day training takes a lot of energy, and we did it live for 18 months straight. For me, every hour of training feels like an hour of working out in the gym. I really throw myself into it! Because it's so draining, we created a hybrid where some portions are pre-recorded from events in the prior six months, and other portions are live. I tell my audience this and am very up front that some of what they'll see is pre-recorded, and some is live. We set it up so that it isn't obvious which parts are live and which aren't and that the whole event seems live.

In these hybrid events, my emcee is live, and people on my team in the chat answering questions are live. It converts just the same. I mention people's names when I'm live, and my team will let me know the questions being asked and the name of the person who asked it. It's all timed exactly, and my virtual team knows when I'm going to say something or answer a question. When I say someone's name aloud, my team types that particular question in the chat, and with the name of the person I call out. It's magnificent, and this also helps people feel like it is truly live at that moment. Even though I've said, "Hey, some of this isn't live," they totally forget. You want to make it look as live as possible. This hybrid model has worked really well. I'm less exhausted, and people stay engaged.

But keep in mind, before I ever tried a hybrid event using recordings, I did it 18 months in a row of 100% live to perfect the event. Each time a question or objection came up during a live training, I'd modify and adjust the slides and trainings for the next event until the whole presentation was pretty much perfect. And even then, we won't let an event run hybrid for longer than six months before doing another 100% live to change it up and keep it fresh. We also do a fully live event anytime a world event happens that can affect conversations or questions in our prospect's mind so we can address them. So, every 4-6 months or so, I'll do another fully live event to update recorded sections.

If there are changes in the industry or hot topics, that's a sign that you need to re-record so it's more up to date and relevant to what's happening in your market. For example, in my real estate virtual event, when interest rates went from 3% to 6%-7% and higher, and we had a massive lack of inventory as well as a possible recession, that was a huge shift. I had to respond to those changes, and bring up those topics, and show how they could outlast any fluctuation in the market. So, I did a new live event including those issues. The more relevant your content, the more you'll convert. The more you speak directly to people's pain points, the more you'll convert. The new live event spoke directly to the pain points of the real estate market: high-interest rates, low inventory, and outlasting tough economic times.

Another factor in the stay rate is the chat. It helps the participants feel like we're a community and that they aren't just sitting at home staring at a laptop. If the chat is active and positive, it helps people stay engaged. It also helps you, as the presenter, to respond in real time to your audience. For me, it's hard to stand in front of a camera for three days straight with no audience interaction, so the chat helps keep my energy up. The key here is to keep the chat upbeat and positive. Weed out any negativity early on! The Negative Nellies never get better; they just get worse and more critical! I have someone on my team monitoring the chat so they can respond to questions, feed me comments, and make sure the disruptive people are cut off quickly. We address negativity at the very beginning of the event and let them know we will immediately kick them off. The needs of the many outweigh the needs of one. And we know how weeds grow fast; we don't want people hurting the success and results of others.

We also let them know if there are any poachers in the group to please let us know. Often, people who have their own programs will go to other people's events and try to private message people attending. We let them know how unethical that is, and if someone does that, to let us know. We also let them know that it's a huge red flag that they would never want to work with someone who is that unethical. My emcee does a good job with this saying, "Imagine if you held an open house, and you invested in ads, you put all this work in, send out flyers, and did a digital campaign. Then, imagine if another agent was on the driveway handing out their card. Wouldn't you be upset? Well, that's like poaching." She reminds them I invested a lot to be here, so please, no poaching or talking about other people's products in the chat. You'll need to come up with a poaching example that makes sense to your Ideal Client. I have the emcee do this because it's a weird subject to talk about, and I don't want that negativity coming from me.

Another thing that causes people to drop off a virtual event is technical issues. You're bound to have them at some point, but if you prepare your audience, people can be patient. I tell my people that if anything happens, just use that time to send a couple of video texts (a strategy I've taught them). I also have an emcee who comes on during any tech issues in the studio. She provides the audience with an update on what's happening and opens up the Zoom to get people to engage. For example, she might ask them what strategy made the most impact on them, or what was an "ah ha" moment for them, or what $75k idea they are going to implement.

Of course, stay rate has a lot to do with your content. It has to be great, not just good. It has to be high value and keep them engaged. They have to see how they can use it in their business or personal life to make a huge difference. You don't want to be teaching a bunch of stuff that they already know. Give them new ideas and perspectives. You've also got to get a feel for the balance between teaching *how* to do something versus *what* to do.

Lever #4: Eyes on Pitch

Sometimes, I use the word "pitch" to teach our 7 Levers for 7 Figures, but I really don't like the word and *never* use it during the training! I'm telling the students in my MDMM group to call it My Irresistible Life Changing Opportunity. "Pitch" always sounds like some sleazy guy trying to sell you something you don't really want or need. I always use the word "offer" because that's how I feel about it. I'm offering to help them get what they want. I'm offering to serve them. It's not just semantics. It's honestly the way I feel about it. It truly is an Irresistible Life Changing Opportunity that I'm offering.

Obviously, if they don't stick around to hear about my offer, they can't accept it and get my help. So, it's critical that they are present during this part of the training, not off getting a snack or responding to their emails. Ideally, you would want the HIGHEST number of viewers on Day 2, right before you go into your offer. Right before your offer is when you need to present your juiciest, knock-their-socks-off, totally compelling training. We always have a really important training that's really going to wow them like crazy right before we make our offer. Also, all aspects of this training showcase what they will get when they invest in my offer. We seed all of the pieces that they need to be successful during this juiciest training (and during the entire three days), and they are a part of the offer I make right after.

For example, the juicy content I present in my real estate events right before my offer is the 9-step process of what to do once a lead requests a market analysis. I've already explained the "What's My Home Worth" funnel to get a prospect to ask for a market analysis earlier in the event. These are the specific 9 things I do to make sure they take it one step further and actually meet with me to sell their home. With these nine steps, their percentage of landing listings will more than double! As part of this 9-step process, I drop off my *Savvy Seller* book, and I drop off a marketing plan. Then, I send this prospect a 17-minute video that shows how I am different from my competitors. I teach people at the event exactly what the nine pieces are and how to use them. Anyone who has been in the real estate business for even a nanosecond can see how valuable these nine steps would be to them.

I really want them to remember the pivotal pieces and the needle movers that could really improve their business. I want them to think, *Oh, my gosh! I need that! It's awesome!* before I make my offer. I need them to know beyond certainty that this will be a game changer in their business if they have what I'm offering. And I need them to know they need me and my step-by-step process to make this happen for them. I want this all to be very crisp and clear in their minds when I'm making my offer. That's why I present it right before my offer. Don't get me wrong. I've also talked about those pieces during Day 1 and Day 3. Remember, you need to *continuously* seed all the pieces of your offer.

Now, how do we make sure they're there to see this juicy content? We tell them it's coming. We use text messaging. Anytime I'm about to do a very pivotal training, or a training is unique—and obviously, right before the offer!— we send a text message that will hook them and grab their attention like, "Hey, you want to make sure that you're here during this time because Krista is going to show you the foolproof system for landing listings" or "Hey, you want to make sure that you're here in the next 15 minutes because Krista is going to be reviewing her XYZ strategy that helped her sell 100 homes per year."

When I'm doing the training, I've already shown them a lot of the pieces of that really pivotal content. I've seeded the *Savvy Seller* book so that my students can be a co-author with me so they have it for their own use. I've already told them that we have the entire format laid out for the marketing plan that our students get. But right before the offer is when I tie all those pieces together and give them more detail. This is where I really bring it home how just these nine steps could make a huge difference in their business. If you do this part right, they'll have to wipe the drool off their keyboards as they reach for their credit cards!

Lever #5: Take Action

This is the ultimate measuring stick for your event. By now, you've helped them prove to themselves how valuable your program would be for them. You've answered their objections and dealt with their limiting beliefs. You've marinated your price by showing them that what they'll gain is so much more than what you're charging, that this investment is worth every penny, and more. You've already given them wins and a number of Ah-ha's that will make a real difference to them. They are totally excited about working with you. And yet, they might still have hesitation.

We'll talk about making the offer itself in Chapter 7. Now let me share some additional tips on how to get them over that hump to take the action they really want to take but are afraid to take. One thing we use to help them prove to themselves how much they need the program is the scorecard (which I'll explain in more detail in future chapters). Basically, the scorecard has them rate themselves on all the things I teach during the event (which are all part of my offer). For example, I'll teach them how to properly distribute videos, and then I'll say, "So, pull out your scorecard and rate yourself on how well you distribute videos." Of course, they rate themselves very low because what I'm teaching is new to them. Then, during the offer itself, I'll say, "Pull out your scorecards and add up your overall score. Can you see that if your business scored higher in those areas, how it would incredibly increase your success?" And I make the connection between everything I've laid out in the offer and what's on their scorecard.

Also, you want to create some urgency. It's too easy to say, "Yeah, this is great, but I'll sign up later." They may have the best intentions, but "later" usually never comes. Create some urgency by offering some time-sensitive bonuses. You'll use them to *monetize* the cost of inaction. For example, we've seen that my co-author book program for *Savvy Seller* is a really hot item for them. (It's a book I've written that is set up, so they can easily add a little to it and join me as a co-author.) We showcase the co-author opportunity and make it a focal point in our morning before the offer. So, I tell them that if they join within the days of the event, I'll include that for free. If they wait, it will cost them $3,000. And that's the truth. I charge $3,000 for the co-author opportunity.

One of my Million Dollar Month Model clients, Wendy, works with businesswomen who want to gain more business from top-level female business executives. They use a bonus of getting people on the cover of a magazine that Elena Cardone was on. "Hey, when you sign up for the program within this event, you're going to get placed on the same magazine cover as Elena Cardone. Can you imagine yourself on the same magazine cover as Elena Cardone, and how that would help enhance your influence?" Then, they tell them that if they wait until later, it will cost them $2,000.

You can also make your intellectual property a bonus. In the future, I'll be offering the CRM I developed as a bonus. I can say, "Hey, right now, if you bought my CRM separately, it will cost you $300 a month. So, by acting today, just that alone is going to save you $3,600." Another bonus might be that those who act quickly get to have a 60-minute one-on-one with you, or they get to have additional accountability calls or additional help from somebody on your staff. (However, I highly advise against that because of time. Once you are selling at scale and getting tons of enrollments, this time commitment would kill both you and your team!) It can be all kinds of things. Just use your imagination. Your goal is to have between three and five bonuses and no more than seven. The idea is that these bonuses are going to be an enhancement to your offer, to your product and service. They will help people get the results they want more quickly. You're giving them a gift of these bonuses because they gave you the gift and the respect to show up to the event and take advantage of your offer.

"Take action" bonuses have to be things that they can't get anywhere else. And it should be something that they can't get without your offer. In many cases, the bonuses would really cost somebody the entire price of the offer if they had to get it elsewhere. You could use bonuses from partners in other industries who are willing to give away a part of their product or service that has a high value. The benefit to this partner is that you're exposing your audience to them and what they're offering as a bonus (which will often encourage your audience to want to work with them more closely).

One bonus I offer to monetize taking action before the event is over is the services of a strategic partner who teaches people how to take all of the tax advantages of being a business owner. One of the biggest things he shows the group is that education is a write-off, so the cost of doing my program is a tax write-off. He also tells them, "You can hire your parents, and as long as they're actually working for you, you can pay your parents and use it as a business expense. If your kids are working for you, you can pay your kids." All these are write-offs that people don't normally think about. He's teaching them something valuable that they can use and implanting the idea, "Wow, I could do these things, and if I did these things, I'm really not even paying for the program." The write-offs he talks about will basically pay for our program or at least a portion of it. (Obviously, I'm not a tax advisor or an attorney, so check with your tax consultant on this.) So, they can either pay the taxman, or they can pay themselves through education and developing their own capabilities. It helps justify the price.

Then, as a take-action bonus, he offers them a free consultation that is valued at $1,300 So, by booking their call, they'll save $1,300 on the consultation and get it for free as our bonus, not to mention tens of thousands of dollars they'll save on taxes. I also remind them at this point that Warren Buffett says the best investment you can make during any time in the economy (especially during difficult times) is investment in yourself through education and investment in your business.

When you bring in an outside partner to add something to your offer, just make sure they are complementary but not competitive. You don't want the group thinking, *Well, I can just work with this other guy and get what I need.* For example, one time, I had this guy who had developed a software that would help people run Facebook ads and pretty much do the ads for them. (I now have developed my own software that does the same thing, basically Facebook ads in 3 clicks!) I was actually teaching people how to do their own ads. And what we discovered is that people thought, *Oh, I don't need all of Krista's program. I'll just go directly to the Facebook software from this guy.* They didn't understand that you really need the entire business model, not just an easy way to create Facebook ads. But people are always looking for a reason or an excuse not to invest. You've just got to be careful about what bonuses you're bringing to the people at your events. If they think it's a cheaper or easier option, they'll do that first and not enroll with you. If you're teaching parenting skills, you don't want to bring in a marriage and family therapist. If your course is about how to become an influencer, you don't want to bring in a PR firm.

At this point, you want to make sure that you answer all the different questions people typically have right after you make the offer. For example, you'll bring up typical questions like, "Is it a one-time payment?" "Yes, it's a one-time payment." "Are there payment plans?" "Yes, there are, but book a call, and we'll go over them." "How many times do we get to meet with Krista?" "Your contract says twice a month, but I do it twice a week because I love teaching." "Will I be able to finish the entire program in one year?" "Well, I can't answer that question because I don't know how much time you're going to put into it. Yes, the entire training was meant to be done in 12 months or less. However, it depends on if you follow our program and model." "How much time is it going to take me every single week?" "Well, I can't answer that either. It's typically between 5 and 10 hours. But some people want to spend 20 hours a week, and some people want to spend three. I don't know how much time and energy you're going to put into this." "How long before I make my money back?" "Again, I can't answer that because I don't know how much effort you're going to put in or if you're even going to do the program." Just think about all the questions people typically have about your program. State the question and give them an answer.

One thing we've discovered the hard (and very expensive) way was that you should only have *one* call to action (CTA). For us, "book a call" has statistically and dramatically been the most successful way for us to get our audience to enroll in our Mastery program. We found when we did multiple CTAs, like "Book a call if you have questions, *or* just go ahead and go to this link and pay in full," conversions went down because the confused mind does nothing. Unless you hate making money, pretty please, only use ONE CALL TO ACTION.

We have found over and over again that if we do *not* allow people to book a call to be able to talk to a live person and ask questions, our conversions go way down. We never *ever* drive traffic directly to a sales link. One time, I had gotten advice from an amazing marketer to send people directly to the "pay now" page, and he apparently had great success in that. Since we test everything, we tested it two different times, and both times, we lost a significant amount of money. The call to action was, "Go directly to the sales link, and you can pay." We generated $367,000 worth of registrations doing it this way one time. But, based on the number of people with eyes on the pitch and our typical take-action rates, we lost at least *$903,000* that month in conversions! So, it doesn't mean that the advice was wrong, but for my audience, it didn't work. And from my experience dealing with multiple coaches, in most cases, especially on virtual events, if they don't have the ability to talk to somebody, your conversions will go down. People just didn't feel comfortable going straight to a link and plunking out $24,000.

Your audience might be different. But whatever CTA you choose to test, just do *one* at a time so they don't get frozen in confusion. Once you have made the call to action, put the URL on every slide thereafter. Don't make them have to look it up. Make it as easy as possible.

Skin In The Game Accountability Program	$1299 value
7-Figure Blueprint Private Facebook Community	$3467 value
6 Expertly Crafted Real Estate Marketing Funnels	$60,000 value
Plug & Play, Customizable Complete Listing Process	$34,125 value
Marketing Plan, Seller's Guide, Buyer's Guide, & More!	$5,125 value
Copy & Paste, Digital Domination Marketing Campaigns	$9,925 value
12 Months Live Coaching, Accountability & Support	$47,499 value
Intensive Digital Marketing Module Training	$19,554 value
Charisma Hacking Training	$9,995 value

$190,989 Total Value

KristaMashore.com/LevelUp

Make sure your technology is working and is very user-friendly because people use every reason imaginable to not say "yes" to themselves. For example, if they try to book a call and the calendar link is broken, or they try to pay directly, and they keep getting error messages, they think, *Oh, that was a sign from God that I shouldn't sign up.* No, there wasn't a sign from God; the calendar link was just broken, or the payment software was glitchy. So now, during my offer, I'll say, "Hey, you might be wondering if you go to the calendar link and it's broken, you might be thinking that this is a sign from God that you shouldn't do that. No, it's just the calendar link is broken, and try again later."

Get them to take action and book within 24 hours because Days 2 and 3 and the two days after the event are critical for calls. You want to catch them before the excitement wears off and they start overthinking it. Remember how we talked about belief and how quickly people lose it? The longer it takes someone to jump on a call, the less you will convert. For example, we can track that after 48 hours, our conversions go down, and no-shows on calls go up because that's how quickly their belief leaves them.

I'll also make sure they know that the call that they're booking is important. "Hey, we know your time is valuable, and so is ours. And so please, when you book a call, please make sure you show up. If you're not going to show up for any reason, please cancel because we have limited staff on hand to answer questions. If you schedule and don't show up, my staff could have used that opportunity to help somebody else. But you're keeping them from doing that by not canceling. So please, if you commit to a call time slot, keep it and show up. You owe it to yourself. But for any reason, if you cannot make it, please let us know so we can have the opportunity to help someone else."

After the offer, we break for lunch so people can book their calls. During that time, we offer an optional behind-the-scenes tour so they can see everything that our students have access to. Our coaches and accountability team are there live to answer program-specific questions and describe what they're seeing. Some people really want to see what's included and actually see the backend. Our coaches pull back the curtain so they can see the program, their training modules and what they get in the modules, where they sign in, the calendar, how to request getting their videos edited, etc. Then we run a loop of student testimonials to help them believe that they too could have the success others have achieved.

When you do this, please be very careful not to get too caught up in "what they get" that's included in your program. Focus on the benefits and the outcomes during the tour and during the entire event. Get them to envision themselves in their desired outcome. Jason Fladlien (who is my new marketing crush, friend, and mentor) says how important it is to get them to see the benefits of what will happen when they invest in themselves and how doing your program will change their lives. He also talks about how important it is to bring up the scarcity side of it and what will happen if they do NOT take action.

Right after lunch, we have our Top Producer panel because you want to give really high-value content after lunch. These are our highest-performing students who have really taken the ball and run with it. I introduce them by saying, "Hey, these people are doing what I'm teaching. You can ask them any question you want." So, they're basically giving a testimonial about the program, but they're also really helping people and telling them what they're doing that's working for them, what they do that has given them the biggest results. That's high value because they're giving them actionable tips, and they're telling them what's working in their business. They all have great stories and amazing insights to share. People can ask them questions and get some awesome ideas and strategies. The panel serves a dual purpose: It's a valuable teaching for event participants, but it also acts as powerful testimonials.

Lever #6: Enrollments

I've talked about the importance of having them book a call as the call to action. You need to have staff who can answer those calls. As I'll discuss in Chapter 4, you need a good, well-trained sales team.

The main thing about this team is that they have to *serve, not sell.* Sound familiar? Your sales team has to really be interested in helping prospective clients get what they want and need, and the team needs to sincerely believe that working with you and your program is how that can happen. To find out what prospective clients want and need, they have to listen—a lot! I always remind my sales team if they find themselves talking or opening their mouths to speak, "You need to ask yourself this one question: 'Why am I talking?'" The salesperson should be doing way more listening and asking questions that get the client to talk. Because the best sales call is when the client actually convinces *themselves* that they need help, not when the salesperson tries to convince them that they do. And based on the questions that they ask and the responses callers give them, each sales call is going to be completely unique. The call should be based specifically on what the caller perceives as their area of weakness, the place where they need the most help to get what they want. Our salespeople find out that information by asking questions that aren't just yes or no questions but open-ended.

One tool I'll teach you in Chapter 5 that has been amazing is our scorecard, which has basically everything that is in our program. Early on during the event, I'll introduce it and have participants score themselves as we go along. Throughout the first day and a half, I'll teach about something that is on the scorecard and ask them to score themselves as to whether they have that in place or not within their own businesses. It keeps them engaged during the event by giving them something to do. It also keeps their brain in the realization of, "Wow, I am really bad in this area. I need help." Typically, 90% of the things mentioned on the scorecard are things they are *not* doing or don't have in place. Every time I ask them to score themselves, they see for themselves how much they are lacking in their current business. I bring the scorecard up again right before I make my offer. "Grab your scorecard, and what's your overall score on X?" They are reminded again of all they are missing.

When they go on the sales call, my sales team says, "Hey, how did you do in your scorecard? What area would you say was the biggest area of weakness?" The salesperson will then hone in on the biggest areas of weakness. "Well, tell me more about that. How long has that been happening? Oh my gosh, what's going to happen if it keeps happening? What does this cost you? What will it cost you if you don't change it?" So, we're getting the callers to see themselves, to admit on their own just how much help they need, and just how negatively it's impacted their life or business.

But if the salesperson talks too much, the client will never get there. The salesperson will never have the opportunity to dive deeper because they didn't ask the right probing questions to lead the client to their "Aha" moment, where they sell themselves on why they need our help. The team will also ask them things like "What got them to sign up? What motivated them to book a call? What did they need more clarification on?"

Lever #7: Follow-Up and Continuing Engagement

Your job isn't over when the event ends. Follow-up and continuing to engage those who didn't enroll is critical. We've gained $300,000 to $400,000 in enrollments based on follow-up after an event. Our enrollments trickle into the next month, but they still came from that event, and our follow-up. We only keep replays of the event available until Friday (2 days after the event), but we continue to text, message, and chat with people who attended. We ask for their feedback, and we encourage them to book a call. We invite them to take a private tour of the program. We also add them to our weekly email list and continue to nurture them, put more offers in front of them, provide more value, and invite them back to future webinars and events. There is power in being a resilient presence for them. People have actually attended 3-5 events before enrolling!

The Feedback Loop

After every event, my leadership team from sales, marketing, and the event team get together and assess *everything* we did that month so we can optimize it for the future. We try to do this within a few days and then again the following week because our sales manager is on calls in the days right after the event. But we want to discuss what was good and bad as soon as possible so we can make changes immediately. You'd be shocked at what you forget. On a 3-day event with hundreds of slides and tons of content, things get forgotten and slip through the cracks easily. So, the quicker you can do an event optimization recap, the better. I had to learn this the hard way.

We track calls booked and calls confirmed versus canceled or rescheduled. Based on feedback from our sales team about calls they had, we look at how clear the messaging for the offer was and look for common questions or objections so we can add them to next month's offer. We look at the average enrollment value, what programs people enrolled in, and how many people paid in full versus went on payment plans. We're always evaluating paid versus unpaid attendees (in a recent event, 88% of enrollments came from paid attendees) and looking for the sweet spot for what to charge for the event. Based on all of this data, all of my teams (including me) look at what they could be tweaking or improving to get a better result.

Based on this evaluation system over the months, we've done things like changed our offer, added and removed trainings and bonuses, changed our event price, removed the fluff from our hub because it inhibited conversions and show-ups. We've changed what we included in our upsells in our funnels prior to the event, and we've changed what gifts we sent them. You can only optimize what you track, and we track everything. What you track will grow. What you don't track will not.

MDMM Mindset: Own Your Results

Once you see the results you're getting, you need to own them! If you aren't getting the results you want, you can't sit around blaming the economy, your competition, the weather, or the alignment of the stars. You can't waste time feeling sorry for yourself or down on yourself. In NLP, they always say, "There are no failures, just results." You just need to take responsibility for whatever results you're getting and make the necessary changes to improve those results. Remember that famous quote? "Insanity is doing the same thing over and over and expecting different results." Einstein may or may not have been the one to say it, but it's still genius!

Take a look at your current business. Where are you getting results that you want, and where are you getting results that you don't want? Where are you blaming external factors rather than taking responsibility for the results that you don't want? What have you been afraid to change that might be holding you back? What could you do differently to improve your results?

CHAPTER 3

First Steps in the Million Dollar Month Model

Later in the book, I'll discuss the operational components of having a Million Dollar Month business. But first, we need to focus on certain aspects of the client acquisition and conversion framework. You may already have a good coaching program or a terrific high-ticket offer. But you won't get to a million dollars per month without a *lot* of clients. Much of what I'll be showing you in this book is how to get those clients. Also, how to set up your program so that it's sustainable and you can keep the clients you enroll.

I'm going to start you off at 30,000 feet so you can get a sense of the pieces and how they'll fit together. It might seem confusing or overwhelming at first. But when you take it step by step and break it down, it won't seem so intimidating. When I started my first coaching business, I had no clue about any of this. "What the heck is a sales funnel?" "You're supposed to track what?!?" It took me some time to really get it, but now it all seems second nature. That will happen for you too, so don't stress over it.

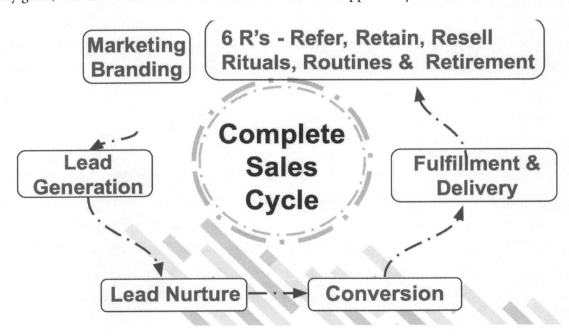

In this book, we're going to focus mainly on the first stages of the Customer Relationship Cycle (Awareness Marketing, Lead Generation, Lead Nurturing, and Conversion) and how we do it in the Million Dollar Month Model. I'll go over some aspects of Fulfillment that will help your program be successful, but I'm assuming that you already have a good sense of the program or product you want to offer. If yours is a coaching business, I'm also assuming that you've had some experience or training in being a coach. Most people who approach me have coaching skills and a great product (or a great idea for a product), but they just don't know how to build it into a great business. They don't know how to scale or monetize it. I teach them how to do that and how to create high-ticket offers out of what they are already offering.

If you're totally new to marketing, that first phase is just getting your name and brand out there. You want people to think of you whenever they think of your industry or your service. You'll find more on this in Chapter 8.

The second phase, lead generation, is more targeted to identify people who could use your product. Now, let me be very clear about one thing: Not all leads are created equal! You don't just want leads. You want *qualified* leads. Qualified leads are not just people who *could* use what you offer. They're people who *want* and *need* what you offer. They may not be ready to buy this very second, and that's okay. But a qualified lead is much more likely to become a client than just any old lead. People think they can take a shortcut and buy leads. You might have some luck buying industry mailing lists, but personally, I do much better generating my own by using the strategies I'll show you. My students say the same.

Once you have qualified leads, you need to *nurture* them. It depends on the program you want to offer, but typically, the investment into coaching is a hefty one for most people. It's not like buying a book for $12.99 or a video download for $24.99. It's easy for people to justify those small amounts to themselves but higher ticket items require more careful consideration. So, potential customers need time to get to know you, to trust and like you, and to see you as the authority in what you're offering them before they'll buy. They need to see you as different and not just doing what everyone else is doing. You truly have to have a unique selling proposition which positions you as "the best and only option out there." And that's what the nurture process does for you.

Conversion is when this qualified, well-nurtured lead (aka a potential client) is ready to buy, and you make your offer. We'll talk about your offer and how to present it in more detail in Chapter 6. For now, just know that this is the part of the process where you might get uncomfortable, *especially* if you don't have rock-solid conviction that your product will benefit them and is totally worth whatever you're charging. Or you might feel uncomfortable if you are upping your offer to a higher ticket price or if you are newer to high ticket offers and programs. Don't let that discomfort/limiting belief get in the way.

All of these steps happen within the Million Dollar Month Model, and for each piece, there are things you can do that will make it more—or less!—effective, which we'll be discussing in detail. As an overview, to build your MDMM business, you start with three "touches" that lead to a free 5-day challenge (I called mine the *5-Day Accelerator*) or a few free 90-minute webinars (I call mine *What's Working Now*). Because program titles can hit marketing fatigue, I change mine up from time to time. I've used *3 Clients in 30 Days: The Accelerator, Unstoppable Agent, Master Sales Persuasion Series*, etc. You get the drift. Even if you present much of the same material, just get creative about the titles. These are trainings that are meant to blow their minds with tons of value. Both models work, but the 5-day challenge started to wear me out, so I switched to intensive 90-minute webinar trainings and our results have been about the same. The 5-day or 90-minute trainings leads them to a relatively inexpensive 2-3 day virtual event (right now, I call mine a Bootcamp). Your offer to join your coaching or training program happens during this 2-3 day virtual event. Personally, as I'll explain later, I've found the 3-day event is better in terms of conversions than the 2-day. I learned this from Bari Baumgardner.

Don't worry, I'll break down each of these events in more detail in later chapters. For now, just get a sense of the overall sequence of the Million Dollar Month Model. But before we get into any part of your marketing for these events, you need to lay some groundwork. First, you need to know who your potential customers are.

It All Begins with Identifying Your Ideal Client

In any type of marketing, you can only be effective if you know the client you're trying to attract. Notice that I said, "the client you're trying to attract," not "the client you're trying to chase down!" In this approach to marketing, your goal is to *attract* people to your program. It's set up so that *they're chasing you*, not the other way around. You want them to be as eager to work with you as you are to work with them. And for that to happen, you have to know who your Ideal Client is.

I have all my students create an avatar (which is like a representation) of their Ideal Client and keep it in front of them as a guide for all marketing decisions. You've probably heard this before, so you will be tempted to not take it seriously, or you think you've already done it. If you think you've already thought about your Ideal Client, so you can skip this section, think again. I've worked with so many experienced entrepreneurs making millions of dollars a year. And I've found that one of the main reasons they are making millions a *year* and not a *month* is that they do not dive into this deep enough. They skim the surface and don't do the work needed to truly identify *all* aspects of their Ideal Client. I can almost guarantee you from my experience 97% of people have not gone deep enough and need to take this super seriously. This process should take you a few days. Yes, days to complete! If you take the time now, you'll save so much time later and make so much more money. Here is a copy of my Ideal Client Worksheet you can use (Theprovenmodel.com/resources).

Scan this QR code using the camera app on your phone to access your resource page & added freebies now!

Creating an Ideal Client is more than just knowing the demographic profile of your ideal client (age, marital status, income, and education level). It's getting inside the heads and hearts of those Ideal Clients. It's their *psychographics* as well. You need to know their attitudes, their beliefs (especially the beliefs that might be holding them back from getting what they want in life), their aspirations, their basic mindset, their thoughts, and their values. You want to know what keeps them up worrying at night. What they love and what they hate. Where they like to shop and *how* they like to shop. Their goals. The vision they have for the life they'd love to create for themselves and their families. What frustrates them, and what makes them excited? You should know your Ideal Client like you know your best friend. You know what they're thinking, and you could almost finish their sentences for them.

For example, let's say demographically, your client is female, 25-35, single, has a college degree, a corporate job, and makes between $35,000 to $50,000. Good start, but then you want to know her psychographics as well. You want to know things like she aspires to own her own sustainable business someday. You want to know that she's a health nut who runs 5 miles every day and scrolls Instagram looking for healthy recipes. You want to understand that she's afraid to take a leap into her own business because she might lose her stable job and its benefits. You want to know that she'd rather listen to a podcast than read and that she wishes she had more time for a social life. And all of this is important because when you know these things, then you know where and what to market to them. You'll know how to hook them to be invested in your content, and you'll get them saying to themselves, "Gosh, she really knows me."

It helps to name your Ideal Client and then ask questions like, "What would (name) think?" "What would (name) want?" "What holds (name) back)?" "What is (name's) biggest problem that is keeping them up at night?" "What is (name's) biggest fear?" (I'll give you a longer list of questions to ask later in this section.) When you put a name to your Ideal Client, they come more alive, and it's easier to imagine how they feel and think.

It's this psychographic information that will give you the insight and ammunition you need throughout the Million Dollar Month Model. With psychographic information, you know where to find them online. You can show up where they are, and you know what will catch their attention. You know so much about them that they feel that you really understand them. And don't we all like and trust someone who really understands us as opposed to someone who doesn't? It's very powerful. If you want people to pay attention and not just scroll past you, you need to market and speak to a specific *person*, not just "the market." I don't care how awesome your program or product is; it's *people* who will make you money, not your offering. Understanding your Ideal Client is not only essential to marketing effectively, it will also help you know how to truly serve them and get them where they want to go.

Research shows that the more your messaging speaks *directly* to someone, the more likely they will convert. So, the more you know who your Ideal Client is, the more you can speak directly to them. Often, my students will even tell me, "I feel like you are talking directly to me." And that's *exactly* how I want them to feel. They feel this way because I know exactly who they are, what they want, how they feel, what they need, what holds them back, etc. Once you've identified your Ideal Client and their pain points as well as their dreams, it makes it so much easier to find ways to serve them and give them value in your trainings, events, and offers.

Psychographics versus Demographics

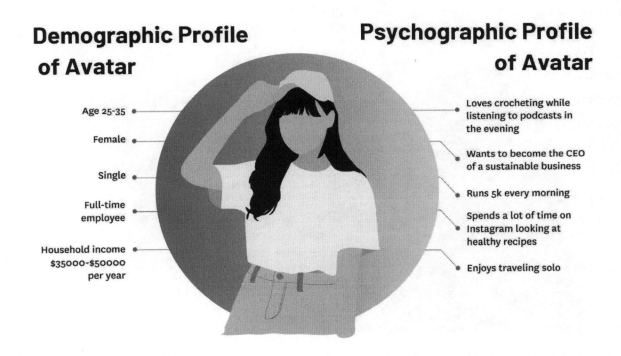

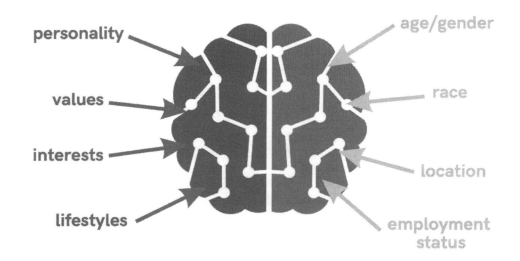

Does this mean you'll never attract people who don't fit the specific description of your Ideal Client? Of course not! When I started, 99% of my clients were female real estate agents. As my business grew, I started attracting mortgage lenders and male real estate agents. It's just how the business grew. But if I hadn't created an avatar of my initial Ideal Client, I would have wasted a ton of time and money marketing trying to "attract everybody"—which would have translated into attracting *nobody*. It's like that old saying, "Jack of all trades. Master of none."

Stacey
40 Years Old - Married

3 years in the Real Estate Biz

Feels like she doesn't have enough time in the day/ overworking

She wants to spend more time with her family/husband. She wants to be financially independent.

She wants to travel, buy her dream luxury items, and get her time back.

People are attracted to you when they feel that you truly understand them, their pain, their fears, their hopes and dreams. They're attracted to you when they begin to like you and trust you. They're attracted when they see that you recognize their problems and have solutions for them. They're attracted when they feel that you believe in their dreams and can support them. To get to that point, you have to know your Ideal Client intimately.

For many coaches, that isn't hard because we were in their shoes at one point. I worked in the trenches of real estate for 17 years, doing all the things that other agents do. I started out having the same concerns and problems (unreliable cash flow, working crazy hours, not having time for my family, etc.). But I figured out how to overcome those challenges and become one of the Top 1% of Realtors® in the nation with a steady 7-figure income. So, I know what they're facing, and I know what will get them to the other side.

It's the same when I started training coaches or people with high ticket offers to build Million Dollar Month businesses. I actually had been where they are, starting from scratch in my real estate coaching and not really having a clue about how to build a coaching business or make a high-ticket offer. I started with zero clients. I spent money in the wrong places and money in the right places. I tried different things that bombed and other things that were pure gold. I went to seminars, read books, and spent literally over a million dollars to train with the best in the business. And today, I'm in the Top 1% of coaches in the U.S. (According to Salary.com, the average business coach in California made just $97,493 as of January 2023. The income range typically falls between $82,186 and $118,891.[1]) In fact, I'm actually 10xing my business this month so I'm in the Top .0001% of coaches!

So, when I created the Ideal Client for my new business—training coaches to build lucrative coaching businesses—I knew *exactly* what issues they'd be running into and problems they'd face. I've been in their shoes. I also now know the solutions and strategies that will help them succeed because I spent the last six years doing it myself. As importantly, I know all the things I did *wrong* and how to steer people in the right direction from all the massive failures I made along the way. (You're welcome.)

In a way, I've been like my own Ideal Client in both businesses: a smart, hard-working entrepreneur with a service mentality who has succeeded in my career and who now really wants to help people find the same success that I've found.

And maybe that's true for you as well. Maybe your perfect Ideal Client is actually *you* from 5 or 10 years ago. For example, if you're working with married couples, maybe five years ago, you were on the verge of divorce, so you know what that pressure feels like and how scary it is. You know what it's like to still love someone but always be in conflict. You know the worry of how it's affecting your kids. You've been in the same boat, so you know what your Ideal Client wants and needs, their dreams and their nightmares. And you found or developed techniques and strategies to successfully get to the other side.

Or it might be that you've *never* been in their situation. You're launching a program about having a great marriage because you've had a great, fulfilling, happy marriage for decades, and you know what makes it work. In that case, your Ideal Client isn't you, but it might be couples you've helped in the past or couples you've known who are unhappy. In this case, for you to really understand your Ideal Client,

---

[1] https://www.salary.com/research/salary/recruiting/business-coach-salary/ca

you'll have to get good at using your intuition and imagination: What do you think they worry about? What are their biggest fears? What do they really want out of life?

Getting clear on your Ideal Client is a critical part of the foundation you need to build your business, so don't take it lightly. Use the following questions to go more in-depth with your Ideal Client:

1. What do they do? How much do they make?
2. How do they feel about their job or business?
3. How do they spend their week?
4. What's their schedule like? The flow of their days/nights?
5. Do they have certain routines?
6. What do they do outside of work?
7. What's their family or relationship status?
8. What are their information sources?
9. How do they stay educated?
10. What happened in their life to lead them up to this point?
11. What keeps them up at night?
12. What are they afraid of?
13. What are their top 3 daily frustrations, roadblocks?
14. What do they secretly desire?
15. What's their current situation?
16. Why is their current situation painful or emotional?
17. Why is their desired situation better than their current situation?
18. What's blocking them from reaching their goals, desired outcomes?
19. How would they describe the things blocking them?
20. What lies or false beliefs are they believing?
21. Why are they believing those lies or false beliefs?
22. What history do they have for their limiting beliefs?
23. What are their pains and problems?
24. What are their dreams, desires, hopes, wants, needs?
25. What aspects of their life and/or personality can you identify to help you market to them?
26. What products are they already buying, and what trainings are they already attending (if any)?
27. What problems do they still have?
28. How can you sell your Ideal Client exactly what they *want* and give them what they *need*?
29. Why would they be interested in your training/coaching/ product?
30. What about your training/coaching/product would make a big difference in their lives?
31. What thoughts, risk-analysis goes through their heads while deciding whether to register for your training/coaching/product?

We also need to ask things like, "Where do they hang out? What do they like to read? What Facebook Groups or Forums do they attend? Who do they follow on social channels? What intrigues them? What would make them stop the scroll?" I know this all seems like a lot, but the reason you are reading this book is because I took the time to figure all of this out. Yes, it took me time to do this, but down the road, it saved me hundreds of hours and will make me millions of dollars. By taking the time up front, I knew where to focus my marketing dollars and what my marketing messaging should be.

Understanding Your Competition Inside-Out

The next piece you need to do for your MDMM groundwork is to really know your competitors. Why? Because you can learn so much from them. People joining my trainings often tell me they know their competition and have this piece covered. But they don't, at least not at the depth they need if they want massive success. It's not enough to know *who* your top competitors are. You have to dig in and analyze what they're doing well and what they aren't doing well. I call it "stalking your competitor," gathering all the information you can about them so that you know them almost as well as your Ideal Client. If you take this seriously and do your research, it will take some time, but it will save you a ton of time and energy in the long run. It will also save you money and *make* you money if you take this seriously.

What if you're not sure who your competitors are? When I started coaching real estate agents several years ago, my competitors were obvious. I knew a lot of the people out there who were training agents, and I'd even taken courses from some of them. I knew exactly what they offered and how they were marketing. Most of them were teaching old-school real estate techniques, so I knew I had something very unique to offer. But when I started coaching people in the Million Dollar Month Model, I didn't know anyone who was in this exact same space. So, I chose high-ticket coaches and trainers who were targeting a similar market and used them for my research.

You may have to do the same, though I bet if you just go online, you'll find someone in your category. I did a quick search and found coaches for parents of autistic children and dementia coaches who work with families and caretakers of people with dementia. I found coaches for accountants, attorneys, dentists, and homemakers. I found psychic coaches, fitness trainers for seniors, and fitness trainers for toddlers. If your high ticket offer is a product (like software), it's the same process. There's everything out there! (But don't let that intimidate you. By the end of this book, you'll know what to do to stand out from the crowd.) Find three competitors that you think most closely offer what your Ideal Client is looking for. (By the way, even though you could learn from a competitor who is failing, you're better off using competitors who are succeeding for this process.)

What Do They Offer?

Begin with finding out all you can about what each competitor offers. What service do they provide, and how do they provide it? What is their core program, and what kinds of bonuses or other programs do they offer? What specifically are they teaching? How much do they charge? Do they have payment plans? Do they offer money-back guarantees?

When you have the answers (as best you can) to these questions, ask yourself: What do you like about their program, and what don't you like? What pieces do you think they are missing that you could provide? What opportunities have they left on the table? How is your approach different and better? You want to create an offer that *far outshines* their offer. In fact, you want your bonuses alone to be better than their core program!

Their Positioning

How are they positioning themselves? For example, when I was in real estate and the market tanked for a couple of years, I positioned myself as the Foreclosure Queen. Later, when the market got better, I positioned myself as a master at marketing high-end homes for sale as the Digital Marketing Queen. When I started my coaching business, no one was teaching agents how to become expert marketers using digital marketing and social media, so that's how I positioned myself. What angle are your competitors using to position themselves in the marketplace? What is their unique sales proposition? What promises and product claims are competitors making? What results or benefits do they say they'll help customers get? What do the competitors' testimonials say about them and their service? For example, do customers say that their service was very responsive or that they got more than they paid for? Do the testimonials mention that other companies failed them somehow, but this one was great?

Now, look at all the information you've gained from these questions. Again, what do you like about how your competitors position themselves, and how could you be different? What do you want customers to say about you that they don't say about anyone else? How can you differentiate yourself and your unique sales proposition from others? What niche or category are they missing?

Their Marketing

Next, dive in and hunt for all the places your competitors market themselves: social media sites, their own website, and industry trade journals. Look at their headlines. What themes do they use? List three common themes you might be able to use in your own marketing. How do they reflect the pain points and aspirations of your target market?

Do they mainly use written copy or video? What other vehicles do they use to market (like books, blogs, webinars, or podcasts)? Check out their sales pages and their landing pages. Are they using anything unique that you could use? Take detailed notes on your competitors' top ads. Notice all the hooks and headlines they use as well.

The point of this is that you want to emulate what they're doing well. That doesn't mean you plagiarize and steal their material word for word! That's not ethical, and it's not effective in the long run because it damages your credibility. Another real estate coach on YouTube literally took an entire training of mine, 100% including the graphics and everything, just changed one word and basically presented the training as his own. That was just tacky.

A few years ago, another guy (someone who was in a mastermind group I was in) approached me about going in together to teach people how to put together successful coaching businesses. He hadn't achieved nearly as much success in the business as I had, but I thought, *Why not?* He came to all of my events, and we did a small training together. But I wasn't liking the way he treated people, so I told him I didn't want to work with him anymore. And right after that, he basically stole all of my material and claimed it was his own! Totally unethical, right? If you're going to use other people's content, you at least want to make sure that you say where you got it from and give credit where credit is due.

And you also need to put your own spin on everything, to put it in your own language and make it yours. But you don't have to totally reinvent the wheel and start from nothing. Leverage off what you discover through your research. As Tony Robbins always says, "Success leaves clues," so it's up to you to find the clues your competitors are leaving. Learn from what others have done well and where they've missed the boat, then apply these lessons to your own business.

You can download a copy of my Competitor Analysis and Ideal Client Worksheet at Theprovenmodel.com/resources.

When you're studying your competitors, I don't want you to get intimidated or compare yourself to them in a negative way. Some of them have more experience. Some of them have bigger organizations. None of that matters. You will find your place and your audience. Because of who you are, you will relate to people and touch people that your competitors can't. There are people out there that *only you* can reach. I was in a coaching with Dean Graziosi, and he said, "You don't have to be better than everyone else. You just have to be better than the you of last week."

Look, I'm cute and blond, I talk fast, and I had a really rough childhood. I'm smart, I hustle and work really hard, and I love great shoes. I'll never wear a three-piece suit or talk like I went to Harvard. But you know what? I know that there are so many people that *only I* can help because of who I am.

That's true for you, too.

You need to teach this to your students and clients. They are unique. They have life stories and ways of doing what they do that no one else has. You should never try to be anything other than who you are because that's your gift. All you need to do is to get better at getting your gift out into the world. All you need to do is get better at being you. Use the information about your competitors to help you do that.

The Big Revelation

The third thing you need to know from the very beginning is your Big Revelation. Think of it like going to a live magic show. The audience is sitting there mesmerized by a magician who is sawing a lady in a trunk in half. But it's only when he shows them how it's all done by mirrors that they think, *Oh my gosh! That's how it works? I never knew that! That's all it takes? I could do that!* That's your Big Revelation. It's an idea or concept that is so powerful to them that their jaws almost drop open. And once you understand what your Big Revelation is, everything else starts to fall into place.

Every business delivers a product, and that product delivers a certain result. The product that delivers a result is your *vehicle*. Your Ideal Client is looking for a product or vehicle that will get them the result they need (whether they know they need it yet or not). Your Big Revelation is the one idea or concept that your Ideal Client needs to believe with 100% certainty and that what you offer (the vehicle) is the *only* thing that can get them the result they need. It's this Big Revelation that gets your Ideal Client to trust and value your solution, your vehicle. Everything you do—from the content of your marketing to your training—needs to connect to that one belief or idea and that it is an *absolute truth*. Your job is to find the Big Revelation.

Most people skip this part. They might mention the Big Revelation, and then they jump right to selling their product. No! You need to be selling your audience on the Big Revelation first and foremost. You need to put all your heart and soul and passion and ethical persuasion skills into helping them believe in your Big Revelation. You need them to be 100% certain that the Big Revelation holds the *key to what they desire*. When you do the Big Revelation part well, they are ready to accept that your product is the *vehicle* they need to get them what they want. But if you skip over the Big Revelation, your audience will still hang on to their natural resistance.

For example, when I started my real estate coaching business, I knew that agents were spinning their wheels and not succeeding because they thought of themselves as salespeople. They knew nothing about marketing themselves, just selling each home as it came along. So, my Big Revelation was: You're not just a salesperson. You're an entrepreneur, and entrepreneurs are expert marketers. This was the *one thing* they absolutely had to believe. They had to believe that their success *depended* on becoming expert marketers. Then, my vehicle was: Expert marketers educate and attract clients through content and video marketing using digital marketing. And that's what my real estate program is all about: teaching them to become expert marketers using digital marketing. My Big Revelation was the thing they had to believe that they needed to get the results they wanted, and my vehicle showed them the only way they could get there.

Big Revelation = *Get Your Audience To Believe This One Thing*
Vehicle = *The Thing That Gets Your Audience To Achieve The Big Revelation*

How about the example of public relations coaching? People who need PR usually have great expertise in specific fields but haven't figured out how to get anyone to notice them. They don't realize that there's a difference between *expertise* and *authority*.

A Big Revelation for PR coaching or training could be: <u>Exposure increases authority, which increases influence, which increases income opportunities.</u>

The vehicle could be: <u>Become an expert communicator and industry authority through attention-collection strategies like being an influencer, social media collaboration, content contribution, social media partnerships, and podcasting.</u>

Make sense? They first need to believe that becoming an authority is the only way to increase income. Then, they need to know that the vehicle for doing this is "attention collection" strategies.

What if you help small business owners scale up their companies?

Your Big Revelation might be: <u>You're operating as a business manager, not a business leader. To grow your business, you must get systems in place to manage and become the leader that a bigger business needs.</u>

Your vehicle could be: <u>Strong leadership, team building, systems, and automation that lets businesses become well-oiled money-making machines.</u>

Your MDMM Brand

You can use all the work you did coming up with your Ideal Client, studying your competitors, and figuring out your Big Revelation to create your branding. Branding is not just the colors on your website or the font you use on a business card. You want your brand to reflect you, what you're about, and how you're unique. It should reflect your values. When people think of you, what do you want them to remember? How do you want them to feel? You also want your brand to connect with your Ideal Client. So, if you're coaching financial planners, your brand might be a little more serious and business-like. If you're planning to coach new parents, the flavor of your brand might be warmer and more friendly, and you'll want to show images that reflect kids and parenting. You also want your brand to help you stand out. For example, there are other people who coach real estate agents, but I'm the only one of the few who can claim to be the Digital Marketing Queen.

Branding is important. It's about how you become known. That said, you don't have to have the perfect logo, or use the perfect font, or have the perfect colors. Brainstorm about your business's name. Make sure no one else has a name that is very similar to the one you choose because it will make it harder for people to find you. Make sure that the name has something to do with the audience you're trying to reach and the results you're helping them to get. For example, Modern Mom Lifestyle is clearly directed at moms and their lifestyles. Seven Figure Real Estate Blueprint is clearly directed at people in real estate who want to make a lot of money.

And if the name isn't perfect at first? Don't worry about it. You'll learn and come up with a better one. When I first made my Facebook group page, I called it Krista Mashore Coaching. That name basically stunk. It was all about me and not about the results I was offering to my Ideal Client. I changed the name to 7 Figure Realtor Blueprint, and we grew to over 2,000 members in a matter of 3 months. People didn't give a hoot about Krista Mashore Coaching, but they were very inspired to join a group that would give them a blueprint for making 7 figures! So, as you brainstorm names for your business, think about ways that what you offer is unique and the results you want your clients to get.

MDMM Mindset: Do It Now!

W. Clement Stone was a businessman and one of the wealthiest men in the mid-1900s. He believed that *delay is the #1 enemy of wealth.* In fact, he would say, "Do it now!" 100 times each day, and he had everyone on his staff do the same. Why? Because taking action is what will boost your confidence. You won't build confidence and your business by just dreaming about the life and business you'd like to have. I always tell my students, "When you feel worried, or tired, or like you just can't handle something, tell yourself, 'Do it now!' If you feel overwhelmed, just say, 'Do it now!'" Inaction leads to doubt, and doubt leads to more inaction. It's a vicious cycle.

Give yourself permission to not get it totally right. Maybe the Ideal Client you create won't be perfect, and maybe you'll miss some of the lessons from your competitors. Maybe your first brand will suck like mine did. *You'll still be much farther ahead because you'll learn from your mistakes if you take action.*

So, just get started and teach your students to do the same.

Spread the Good

What if, in just two minutes of your time, you could really help a stranger to succeed?

And what if, because of your kindness, that stranger is able to help many, many others?

That's what can happen if you give *My Guide to Million Dollar Months* a 5-star review. Your review will encourage someone you don't even know, maybe the next Tony Robbins or Mel Robbins, to read this book and learn how to build a business that makes an incredible impact.

And it won't cost you a thing.

(How to links here)

Thank you!

CHAPTER 4

Create the Vision of Your Million Dollar Month Model Business

For most of my career, I've sought out Million Dollar Coaches. I always wanted to learn from the best of the best, even before I decided to get into coaching myself. And from these Million Dollar Coaches—like Tony Robbins, Jason Fladlein, Russell Brunson—I've witnessed certain things that make them not just good, but great coaches. It's not just the quality of what they teach, though that is really important. It's also the quality of their organizations and how they treat their customers and clients in everything they do. We'll talk more about this throughout the book and what you need for a high-quality organization.

Your Unique MDMM Business

But first, you have to decide what kind of business you really want. I learned very early in my career that you have to start with a clear vision of what you want to get anywhere. If you don't, you end up putting your time, effort, and money in the wrong places. You get caught up in tasks and strategies that steer you in the wrong direction. *A clear vision of what you want acts like a lighthouse guiding your ship. Even when things get foggy or stormy, you can still keep moving toward your goal because of your clarity.*

I'm guessing that you already know what you intend to offer and have some sense of what your program will look like. The question is, how large of a business do you envision for yourself? Is your vision to be a female Tony Robbins? This was how I once stated my vision. My focus was more on the kind of impact he's able to make rather than how much money he makes. Tony's organization is huge and generates way more than a million dollars per month. Is that what you want for yourself?

I teach the Million Dollar Month Model, and if you follow this system, you certainly *can* make a million dollars in a month. But many of my students are happy making $100,000 or $300,000 per month. They prefer a smaller business and a smaller organization to support it. They want to stay more intimate with their students and there's nothing wrong with that. They still follow the MDMM system. They just don't do it at the scale that students who want a larger business do. However, they still have to invest their money, time, and energy to make it happen. You don't earn $300,000 per month with no effort or cash outlay. But the $100,000-$300,000 coaches don't have to invest as *much* money, time, and energy as people who are building larger businesses have to invest. That just makes sense, right?

The level of business you want will also affect many of your decisions. For example, I think personal coaching is great. You just have to understand that if you're doing one-to-one coaching yourself, obviously, the profit margins are very, very different. You only have so much time in the day, and paying others to be coaches for you can get expensive. For a larger business, you would need enough coaches to be able to handle the volume. At this point, I don't offer one-on-one coaching. I used to have one-on-one coaching in my offer, and it was very, very helpful to some people, but it got to the point where it wasn't very profitable or helpful to me. It was too much pressure on me and made me a less effective coach for others. Often, people showed up to coaching calls just to be able to talk, almost like going to a counselor, and they didn't really get stuff done. So, we started doing the group calls for ongoing accountability. We created drop-in office hours where they could show up and talk to somebody to get help. We do this in a group setting because when someone asks a question, it's often a question that others have, and everyone can benefit. We now have eight different drop-in office hours a week. (We do have a one-on-one accountability coach for the first 37 days for new students to make sure they start off right.) This has turned out to be much less expensive. But it isn't just about the money. Group coaching is more effective for students because they get to hear questions that other people ask that they hadn't thought of asking. When they see others in the group succeeding, it helps them believe that they, too, can succeed.

No matter what size business you decide you want, this is still a business, *not* a hobby. You need to approach it like any other legitimate business if you want to succeed.

Your vision for your business will probably change and evolve. But you need a starting place. Here are some questions to help you figure out what you want your business to ultimately look like:

Is what you teach appropriate for teaching in large groups, or would small groups be more effective?

How much time and energy do you want to commit to teaching and coaching personally on an ongoing basis?

How big of a team do you see yourself leading?

How much money are you *committed* to making? Yes, we all would love to win the lottery, but what level of income are you willing to *work* for?

How much time, money, and energy are you willing to commit to building your business?

How much are you willing to grow and change as a coach and as a business owner? How much are you willing to invest in yourself to get the growth you need?

Your Organization

It's not exactly true that "if you build it, they will come." But it's for sure true that if you *don't* build an organization for your MDMM coaching business, they will never come! You need some systems, team members, and structure in place, even in the beginning, no matter what size MDMM business you're building. The truth is, if you want a big MDMM business, you *cannot* do it all yourself. One of my students, Tim, did start that way. He had grown a business where he gave live presentations and workshops, and he had let his private clients go. But when COVID hit, his live presentation business basically shut down, and he was back to square one and left without much in financial resources. So, when he started MDMM, he built all of his own slide presentations, did all the marketing himself, and even answered the sales calls (which I *never* recommend, as I'll explain in a few pages). He told his family that he'd be working around the clock and that he'd be unavailable for about four months while he got the business off the ground. His first event brought in over $103,000 and has grown from there. And now, as his income has grown, he's started to build a team, putting key people in place.

Scan this QR code using the camera app on your phone to access your resource page & added freebies now!

Dan Sullivan always says that it's *who,* not *how,* that will bring you success. Hiring the right people is critical! Hiring people who are not competent or dedicated is a recipe for disaster. For example, when Tiffany first started, she paid someone a bunch of money to handle all of the technical set-up for her webinar and events. In the middle of her first free webinar, she realized he had put up all the wrong links! Rather than links so people could register for her 3-day event, he put up links that went directly to her offer. "I basically lost everyone from that first webinar. From that experience, I've learned to be my own QC person and check everything before my webinars and events. I've also learned how to interview more effectively when I'm hiring and ask better questions as well as checking references rather than being so trusting."

Your Technology

One of the most important pieces is a really good CRM (customer relationship management system) to handle not only your marketing but also to keep track of your business as it grows. You'll be marketing on social media, distributing posts, and placing ads that provide great content (see Chapter 8), so you need a system to track all of the requests and interest that gets generated. You need a system that can follow up with prospects, nurture leads, and keep building relationships, as well as staying connected to current clients to make sure nothing and no one drops through the cracks. You need a system that can handle communication with people who sign up for your events and who enroll in your program. You need a system to send reminders, text messages, emails, etc., and you need to make this automated, or it will be impossible to get the results you want.

I've worked with a bunch of different CRMs, but none of them had all the processes and capabilities we needed. So, I finally ended up bringing in a team and developing my own! It was a huge expense, and by the time it was done, I'd spent thousands and thousands of dollars. But I'll tell you that it was totally worth it (and now I offer it to all of my MDMM students). I don't have to scramble to piece together information from different systems to run my businesses. I can now easily check on how our marketing is doing, track our follow-up, and see our results in one place. I don't have to lie awake at night wondering if we've missed something.

You don't have to start with a state-of-the-art CRM, but you do need a good one in place even in the beginning. Expect to spend some money on this if you don't already have one.

Your Marketing Team

As you saw in the 7 Levers (Chapter 2) and as you'll see even more in Chapters 7 and 8, marketing is a huge piece of building your business and keeping it profitable on an ongoing basis. You need a marketing team that is creative, energetic, analytical, and totally proficient in social media. When I started my first coaching business, I did most of the marketing myself. I was already an expert in digital marketing from my real estate business, and I was known as the Digital Marketing Queen. So, it wasn't too difficult to apply the same tactics and strategies to building a coaching business. But it also meant that I was exhausting myself because I was still running my real estate business.

You might be able to start out doing your own digital marketing. Just know that your MDMM business will grow more slowly. Personally, I recommend to my students that they hire some good digital marketers as soon as possible. Many on my team are virtual (as are many of the different people on my team), some from the U.S., and others are people from the Philippines who assist them. I create content, then they run with it (placing ads, generating posts and emails), and, most importantly, tracking results.

Beyond the digital side of marketing, my team gets me gigs writing articles for online publications that my target market follows. They set me up to be interviewed on podcasts where the audience is similar to mine, like Russell Brunson's, Dean Graziosi's, John Lee Dumas', Brad Lea's, and some other super well-known names. They find and book speaking opportunities for me. All of our marketing efforts are coordinated, and we always track results to make sure we're investing our time and money in the right places.

Again, you don't have to start here, but you will need to invest time, energy, and money into marketing. The amount you're willing to invest will determine how quickly you will grow. And at a certain point, you won't be able to handle it yourself, even if you're a marketing expert.

Your Sales Team

Your sales team will make or break your business! You might think this is an added expense that you can't afford starting out. I don't see it that way because I know the cost of *not* having a good sales team. It's an investment you can't afford *not* to make! One of my students, Anthony, coaches public speakers on how to get more speaking engagements, how to be more effective on stage, and how to build a speaking business. He is an awesome person and a terrific coach, but he was not getting great results in his first couple of months using the MDMM system. We analyzed it and realized that his salesperson was only closing 7% of the people who booked a call at his virtual event. That's crazy! My team closes on average between 47% - 67%, but we've had months where the close rate was up to 87%. With the way the MDMM system works, the sales team shouldn't have to do a lot of "selling" (I'll talk about this more in Chapters 6 and 7). People who book a call are pretty much already sold and just need someone who is skilled in helping them take that last step to say "yes" to themselves. Anthony's guy was not that person.

Anthony was doing exactly what he was supposed to do to get people to say "yes," but his salesperson was letting him down. The guy had been with him for about a year, but because Anthony wasn't doing as much volume before starting with MDMM, Anthony hadn't noticed a problem. Fortunately, we helped him identify the issue within his first couple of months with MDMM so he could make a change and get the right sales team with the right training. As Anthony said, "You never know you've got holes in your bucket until you pour enough water in."

The sales team *cannot* be you, the person who is presenting the event and is the main person of your program. First of all, you can't be on the phone after you make your offer because you've still got another day and a half of the event to lead (we'll go over the timing of making your offer in Chapter 7). Also, the person who is the coach should be a little bit elevated and not so accessible. If you're too accessible to them, it devalues your program and undercuts what you're charging them to have access to you and your expertise.

What do you pay a sales team? Well, some people may disagree with me, but I pay my team salary plus commissions based on gross sales amounts. Since they are getting a pretty good salary, the commission doesn't even start until they've hit a certain threshold. Then, they get paid commissions/bonuses based upon how much they sell in certain tiers after they hit the threshold. A good salesperson (depending on how much your offer is) should make at least $150k a year. Good closers with a good offer can make much more. The better the offer, the better their closing ratio can be. This gives them great potential to make an excellent living. Because people are already sold before they get on the sales call, I don't think that the team should be earning a 10% commission on the sale. The "selling" has already been done by the time they talk to a prospective client. Don't get me wrong. My sales team still has to help push them over the edge, answer questions, and overcome objections. Unfortunately, the wrong salesperson can literally talk someone out of the sale! So, you still need a skilled sales team who believe in you and the product and who can convey that with conviction. My team *is* paid well so that I can hire quality people.

One thing I've learned is if a salesperson is not working out, if their numbers are consistently below the norm for the team or if they don't treat your prospective clients the way you want them to, get rid of them sooner rather than later. They'll start negatively affecting your other salespeople and even giving your organization a bad name.

Your Production Team

When you start out, you may not need much. If you are just a bit tech-savvy, you can record and edit your own videos for marketing. You can run a Facebook Live or Zoom sessions by yourself. When I first started my coaching business, I set up the camera and did Zoom webinars all by myself. I cued the slides and kept track of comments in the chat the best I could, and it worked. But as I quickly attracted more people to my events, I started hiring help.

On my team, I now have 17 full-time videographers. But that is only because, as a service in my coaching programs, we offer video editing to help our students be more successful. Sixteen of these editors are in the Philippines, and I have one full-time person who lives in my city and works closely with me. For my marketing, the team records the videos and edits them to different lengths for different platforms, adding music and graphics and helping with post-production posts on social media. (At the time of writing this book, we are learning how AI can do a lot of this stuff for you. That might reduce the number of video people you'll need. So do your research on that.) During my events, they cover the cameras, switching views and angles. They also run PowerPoint slides and cue up videos and music.

Also, during my events, I have a couple of people on my team who monitor the chat, respond to questions, and post information. They're also available for participants who have technical challenges during the event. I also now have an emcee for my 3-day virtual event. She's responsible for introducing me and handles housekeeping (more on this in Chapter 7).

When I started, I just set up my camera in my office or another area of the house and used Zoom. At this point, I still use Zoom, but I've built a small studio in my home. We just have one camera and software that can show me and my slides at the same time to the audience. (Some of my MDMM students have set it all up so that all they need is a switch that their foot activates so they can do it all on their own.) Our different seminars now typically have 300-400 participants, so I've got eight 60-inch monitors on the walls so I can see them all.

Again, you don't have to start at this level. You can start small and build as you go. In the beginning, when you are first starting out, all you need is you, a $97.00 camera, and Zoom. Don't overcomplicate it. As you get better, as you start making more profit, then you can add TVs and hold your events on different platforms. But really, in the beginning, just you, Zoom, and a $97 Logitech camera that plugs into your computer will be enough. You can get better equipment as you get better, but you just need to start for now. Just be aware that you'll want to invest in your production quality at some point. But even in the beginning, I would recommend that you have someone on your team who can monitor the chat for you during events so you don't get distracted.

Other Team Members

Depending on your business, you might need more people on your team. Some will be paid, and some might be volunteers. For example, I have Accountability Coaches. These are some of my advanced students who run my daily Skin in The Game accountability groups. They volunteer to do this because it's beneficial to them, and they gain more access to me. It also helps them be more accountable to themselves because since they are running it, they have to show up. So, it's a win/ win for everyone. If you'd like to know more about this, click Theprovenmodel.com/resources, and I can show you how Skin in the Game works.

Your MDMM Budget

Compared to many businesses, the Million Dollar Month Model takes much less money to launch. That said, it's still a business. You need to spend money (on your team, technology, advertising, etc.) to make money. And it's important to realize that the money you make on MDMM each month is not cash in hand. Many people will opt for payment plans that can go 3, 6, or even 12 months. So, like any new business, in the very beginning, your expenses will exceed your income. When people start any other kind of business, they get $100,000 or $200,000 to get them off the ground. You definitely don't need that much in the very beginning, but the more you put into it, the faster your MDMM business will grow.

Tiffany's business started having a positive cash flow in the fourth month. The price of her offer is $14,997 or $17,997 if they pay monthly for 12 months. The first three months, she threw almost everything she made back into ads. Here's how she calculated her budget: "If you enroll 20 students in one month and they all go on my monthly payment plan, that's $29,980. I've put about $20,000 into ads each month, plus paid support people as I'm building my team. That month's income compounds, so the next month, we're bringing in $59,960, then $89,940 the following month. So I know what money I have to build my team and increase my ad spend."

Of course, not all students go on payment plans. Some pay in full, which you really want to encourage by offering deep discounts to get cash flow going. You can also use services that finance high ticket offers. It's similar to an enrollee putting it on their credit card. They're making payments on it to the finance company, but you're getting the full amount right away. That said, I personally don't use a finance company. The ones I tried charged a huge commission and hurt us more than they helped us. So be careful about using this as an option.

Leadership

If you want to build a sustainable MDMM business, great leadership is critical. You may or may not think you're a great leader now. But whatever level you're at right now, trust me, you'll need to get better. I could write a whole book about everything I've learned about leadership since I started my business. My biggest learning came just right before I actually started creating and implementing the Million Dollar Month Model in my own business. It all happened within one crazy week.

COVID had just hit, and everything was getting shut down. No more speaking engagements. No more live workshops. The entire business model I had at that time was disrupted. Plus, within that same week, and without any warning at all, both my Director of Marketing and my Director of Human Resources quit. What I didn't know was that they had been in the process of creating their own coaching program while working for me (and I was paying them!) for the prior 12 months. The program they had put together was frankly a bit too similar to mine. To top it off, they also took several of my employees with them.

Just before that, I had been on a vacation in Mexico, and my credit card was shut down. That's when it really hit me that my business expenses were totally out of whack, and it simply wasn't sustainable. For one thing, I was paying my sales team way too much. I tried to renegotiate with them, but they were pissed off and thought I was just being greedy. So, I ended up letting them all go. (Later, I heard from some of them who said, "Wow! We didn't know how good we had it with you back then!")

There I was with my Director of Human Resources and Director of Marketing bailing on me right when I needed them most! I have to say it really hurt. My Marketing Director was pregnant, and I'd made a point to tell her, "Hey, I know your husband's not working. The company is not doing well right now, but I want you to know that even if I have to let other people go, your job is safe. Don't worry. We'll get through this together." Apparently, she had other plans that I didn't know about. (Actually, she called me about six months ago and apologized for what she had done and the way she left.)

My feelings were really hurt, and I have to say I took it personally. But then I started thinking, *Okay, if these people are leaving, I must be doing something wrong. I need to change something I'm doing and get better.* I realized that my students love me and rave about me, but my team members (they're really my team, so I don't call them employees) weren't as happy as they should be. I wasn't leading them the same way I was leading my students.

I made the commitment to myself right then that going forward, every single one of my team members would love working for me and love their jobs. I made the commitment to be a better boss and the best leader ever. I hired a leadership coach. I got all of John Maxwell's books on leadership and read them. And I worked really hard at it. Since then, students and others who work with my team are always saying, "Oh, my God! How did you get such a great team? How come your people are so loyal to you? They'll take a bullet for you, and they all care so much about what they do."

It starts from the top, right? Your company is a reflection of you. So, if you are having a lot of churn and losing people, if your people aren't happy, if you don't have a positive culture within your organization, it starts with *you*. You need to look at yourself before you can look at anybody else. You need to learn to be a better leader. Whether it's good or bad, you can typically tell a lot about a company based on how they treat their people.

For example, the other day, I met with somebody who owns her own business. I could tell she was kind of a rough person, and she started yelling at one of her team members right in front of me. And I realized that years ago, I was similar to that. I didn't actually yell like that, but I think the energy I used was similar. Back then, if an accident or something bad happened, I'd be asking why it happened and finding someone to blame. It's a fear-based kind of leadership. But today, my approach is, "Hey guys, this happened. Now, how do we make sure this doesn't happen again? It doesn't matter who's at fault. How do we fix this? How do we make sure it doesn't happen again?"

I used to work for a guy at Costco who was a dictator leader. He walked around with a scowl on his face. Nobody liked this guy, and people hated their jobs. He liked me a lot, probably because I was a crazy hard worker. In fact, I got the job because I would show up every single day at the Costco trailer until he finally hired me. Because of that, he respected me and used to tell everybody all about me. He wasn't mean to me. He was really nice to me, but I was still afraid of him, and it was hard to watch the way he treated other people. He had a lot of churn. He had a lot of unhappy people, and because he was the main head manager, the managers under him acted exactly the same.

One of the first things I realized as I worked on being a better boss was that I was expecting too much of my people. I was expecting them to treat the company like it was their company. It's not their company. They're never going to work as hard as I work or care as much as I do about it. I had to become more realistic and realize that if all of these people who were my team members were able to do what I had done, they would have done it. They'd have their own companies.

I expect a lot from my team members now, and we have high standards for what we do. But I don't expect them to work as hard as I do. I treat them like family, I respect them and try to support them. For example, recently, one of my top people came to me. She's been with me for two years, and we've taught her everything she knows about marketing. She said, "I want to give a 30-day notice because my health is bad. I didn't find any other job. I just need to take care of myself."

I said, "Okay if it's your health, you don't need to give a full 30 days' notice."

She said, "Are you sure? I don't want to leave you stranded."

I said, "No worries. Just give us your SOPs (Standard Operating Procedures) and meet with the team. We'll figure it out. But do me a favor. Don't give your notice. Take 30 days and see if your health gets better. If you feel better and you want to stay, great. If you say you want to go, great. I'll support whatever you want to do."

Two and a half weeks went by, and she called saying that she wanted to come back. I said, "Is it a money thing?"

She said no but that she had used up her vacation and she really wanted to come back. I told her to take an extra week. I also said, "And when you come back, you need to tell me if anything is stressing you or you need time off for your health." I not only retained a great team member, but she's totally loyal, and she'll never forget how I supported her.

I once hired this consultant to come in and look at every aspect of my company. When he started, he said, "Krista, I hear you say that you guys are a family, but you're not a family. You are supposed to be a well-oiled operating machine, and people need to stick to their role. But you are not a family." But after meeting with my company for three solid days, he said, "You are right. Don't change anything. You guys really are a family, and it actually works for you."

Another thing I've learned is to hire slowly and fire fast. You can't be in a hurry or desperate when you hire. You have to take the time to really check them out, not only their skills but also their personality and work ethic. You need to know that they will be a good fit within the team and that you'll be able to trust them. I've learned that the more somebody is willing to do to get hired, the better they'll be as an employee (team member). We use a hiring funnel where we'll bring people through and ask them to do certain things. We ask them to send a video and tell us about themselves. We'll have them do a specific skill. For example, if I'm hiring somebody to do Facebook ads, we give them a little bit of Facebook training and have them do a specific activity pertaining to Facebook ads. If they're not willing to do those things, they're not going to be very good employees. When I first got my real estate license, I went to the office for four months while I was studying for my test. I just showed up every single day and followed people around, and went on appointments with them. I wasn't getting paid. And after that first year, I was a top producer in the entire office. It's because I was willing to do the work even before I got the job. You would be shocked about how many people go through our funnel and are not willing to even write one page so you can see their work! That's a good thing because they're the ones who wouldn't do the work you need from them if they got the job. When you take your time hiring, you don't waste time training the wrong people.

On the flip side, when it comes to firing, do it quickly! That may sound harsh, but if someone causes trouble with other team members or doesn't do what they say they'll do, or doesn't have the skill set you thought they had, it's best to let them go. When someone isn't doing a good job or has a stinky attitude, it brings the entire team down, and you can't afford that. A friend of mine used to work in a temporary employment agency. Every Friday, a few of the companies that hired their temps would be unhappy and not want the temp to come back. So, every Friday, she ended up having to fire a bunch of people. She hated it, but her boss used to tell her, "On some level, this person knows they aren't doing a good job and they aren't a good fit. What you're doing by firing them is releasing them to find a place where they can succeed." It made the firing she had to do a lot easier.

That said, I've learned to sleep on it if I'm upset about someone or something. I used to get pretty emotional and take things personally. Though I always like to take action quickly, I've realized that when something negative happens, I need to hit the pause button and not react too quickly, maybe even sleep on it. Good decisions never come from a negative mindset. So, I'm careful to get my mindset straight first if it's something that upsets me. I make better decisions, and if I have to deliver bad news, I'm able to do it in a much calmer, clearer way.

This is something I have to work on constantly. I had a meeting recently, and I was getting frustrated because my team wasn't hearing my point. I felt like I was saying the same thing, and nobody was really listening to me. It was just that I wasn't explaining it correctly. But I found myself getting a little frustrated, and I thought, *Why is everybody so quiet? Why isn't anybody speaking up?* Well, it's because I wasn't leading correctly. I wasn't making the meeting seem like a very safe place. They were afraid to speak up because I was already agitated. It wasn't them. It was me. My fault. Once I realized what was going on, I told the team, "Hey, I apologize if I haven't been like normal the past two weeks. I want you guys to feel comfortable in these meetings and speak freely."

A good leader doesn't try to be right all the time. You want your people to bring out things to you that you're missing. You want your team to challenge you and tell you how you can be more efficient and be better. I never want to be the smartest person in the room, and I do not want "yes" people around me. I let my team know, "I always want you to come to me for anything. I might not always agree with you, but I'll always listen. In many cases, I will agree once you've made your point. But at the point where I make a decision, I need to know that you're going to back me 1000%. Once there's a decision made in the company, I expect everyone to support it whether they agree or not."

A good leader is somebody who encourages, inspires, and motivates. A good leader wants to build their people up, not cut them down. It's also important to be direct in your communication, but with kindness. For example, I try to be as clear as I can about expectations and timelines. When I have to talk to someone because they aren't meeting those expectations, I use what's called a "feedback sandwich." In a feedback sandwich, you start with something positive about them, then tell them what isn't going right, and end with something encouraging and positive. For example, "I really appreciate the way that you deal with our students on the phone. (NOTE: Be sure not to use the word "but" here. It negates everything you just said.) I'm a little concerned about the emails you send them because they seem a little too abrupt. I'd like you to be more aware of what you're writing and even have someone read them before you send them to get feedback. I know you really care about our students and want to do the best you can for them." When you do a good feedback sandwich, people don't go on the defensive. They're more open and able to hear what you need from them.

And it's so important to give feedback frequently, not just during annual reviews. You want to correct someone quickly, and you want to praise people often. One rule of thumb is that you *never, ever* give negative feedback in front of others. It's humiliating and makes everyone feel uncomfortable. On the other hand, giving positive feedback in public has all kinds of benefits. First, people work better when they feel good, and who doesn't feel good after getting praise from a boss? The person you're praising feels even more honored because other people heard it. Also, it encourages others to want that feedback for themselves, so they work even harder to get your praise.

Virtual assistants are also part of our family. Several people on my team work remotely, and I now have several amazing virtual assistants from the Philippines. I get them through onlinejobs.ph, and they're very affordable. Sometimes, there's a little bit of a language barrier, but that doesn't mean that they aren't really sharp. Everything that applies to my onsite team applies to anyone working remotely. Like your onsite team, you need to set clear expectations, give good feedback, and show your virtual assistants respect.

Plus, you have to give them quality training. Spend the energy and money to do it correctly from the start so you don't have to keep training them forever. When I hear people say, "Oh, I have terrible virtual assistants," it's usually because they never trained them properly. I'm not the best trainer because I'm just not detail-oriented enough, so I've learned to hire people who are. Each of my team members has created standard operating procedures (SOPs) that describe what they do. We have them record videos, get them transcribed, and keep them in our learning portal for new hires.

Now, with Artificial Intelligence (AI), you can literally record a video of you doing your job and just talk it through. You can make a transcription of that recording (I use Loom because Loom actually has AI in it) and tell it to make the SOPs for this specific job role utilizing this transcript. Then you can say, "Okay, tell me all the areas with this job role that were confusing," and AI will tell you. Next, you can say, "Based upon all of your suggestions, rewrite the SOPs for this job role." It will literally give you every single step of how to do that job with the video attached.

Another thing you need to be aware of is that good people usually need some kind of path for growth in their jobs. My top four or five people all started in an administrative role, and I love hiring within. I know, in principle, that you're not supposed to do that. But it has worked great for me. I always look within my own company anytime I'm hiring for a new position that's needed. I look to see who in the company could do a good job if we just trained them in the skills they need. You can train anything into the right people. A skill can be learned or taught. If it's not the right person, you really can't train them in anything. But the right person can move up quickly in my company. It's not a matter of who has been here longer but work ethic and attitude.

If you asked my team, "What are the company's core values?" I don't think they could tell you. But you see it in everything they do. And those core values come from what you, as the leader, model for them. My team can see my dedication and my passion in really taking care of people and getting full results for them. Those are the values my team emulates. I also insist that people are treated with respect. When people join our community as students, I always tell them, "Hey, please treat my team well. They're like my family. They work hard. They care. Please, please be good to them." But you can't just tell someone to respect others. You have to model it.

There's so much to know about being a good leader that I highly recommend that you study it. As the leader of your company, if something is going wrong, it's typically your fault. You have to look in the mirror and say, "How did I cause that? How could I have made that better, and how can I make that better now? What role did I have to play in that?" By doing that, I've made massive changes in my life and improved my company culture exponentially (not to mention 10xd my company's income!). Just looking in the mirror and saying, "Okay, Krista, what could you do better? What part did you play in that?" has made all the difference.

Troubleshooting Your Business

It's important to know that if you have a lot of churn in your program (meaning people are leaving or want refunds), that's a reflection of the quality of your program or the support and accountability they are receiving. We have added to our program so much over the years. I literally could write a book about things we've done to create such a successful program.

I was at Russell Brunson's Atlas Mastermind, and someone asked me a question. After I answered it, I was told it was the most comprehensive answer and perfect. When the same question was asked to the group, the whole room basically said, "What she said." The question was, "I'm starting a coaching program. What do I need to be thinking about to make it successful?" Here was my answer:

1. *Start with the end in mind.* Make sure that you know how much time you want to put in. Right now, you're excited, and you'll stay that way. But after you've done it for a year or so, you'll realize that coaching takes a lot out of you. You're basically an energy giver, which can and does take a lot of energy from you. Right now, you may think coaching an hour a day isn't a lot, but it is. So, under-promise and over-deliver. If you think you want to coach five days a week for one hour a day (which I don't advise), put it in the contract that they get you two days a week for an hour. Under-promise and over-deliver. That way, if you get sick or get tired or want to go on vacation, you're covered.

Personally, I don't do anything one-on-one. My coaching is all group coaching, which I find more useful. People can learn from one another and hear answers to questions they didn't think to ask. If you're going to offer one-on-one coaching, whether it is from you or someone else on your team, really think that through. It's exhausting and very expensive. You couldn't pay me enough to work one-on-one.

I used to allow my students to have Voxer (it's like a walkie-talkie) access to me. OMG, it was a huge mistake! Most people are respectful and considerate in their expectations. But you always get a few who are not. I had one gal who would message me all hours of the day and night. She abused the privilege. I would be on vacation and kindly remind her that I was trying to enjoy my family. But she didn't care; she would go on and on. And in the beginning, I wasn't strong enough to tell her. I gave her so much of my time and energy just to eventually have her leave the program and basically blame me. It was so crazy. I followed her through the year and watched her use so much of what I had taught her. My point is you need to be careful about how much access you allow.

2. *Having a great success plan for when they first join is essential.* We have each person go through orientation with one of my team members. Now, I know this is the opposite of what I just said about no one-on-one, but it's essential at this point. People have just pulled out their wallets, and they're excited but also nervous. They start to doubt their decision. Remember when I talked about belief and how quickly people lose it? You have to keep re-enrolling them and assuring them that they made the right decision. By over-delivering, answering questions, and reducing overwhelm in the beginning, you're assuring more success later on. It definitely helps with retention rates.

It's imperative that you're just as obsessed and excited about their experience and success once you get them in as you were to get them in. I'm obsessed with my customer experience and their journey, and it shows in my program. We have a Group Orientation as well. My coaches, accountability coaches, and anyone they will have direct contact with, including me, are on that call, letting them know they made a great decision and they are in the right place. I tell them 5-6 things that we see people do that give them the most success in the program. We also have a 37-day quick start program where we hold their hand, give them extra service and support, extra accountability. We have found that if we can get people really involved and experiencing some success in the beginning, they will follow through with what they need to do to get where they want to be. We make sure in the first 37 days to get them some small wins, make them feel comfortable, and answer their questions. They have a personal group they begin the program with. Every single day, they know exactly what to do. They have two extra hours each week of calls with their group to really get them as much success in the beginning as possible. They also have a success accountability coach for the first month. They have a 15-minute call with them every week just to make sure that they're set up for success. This program has been instrumental. I wish I had done that earlier because it's been a game changer.

Another thing we learned along the way is to anticipate the challenges and obstacles people will hit along the way and address them early on. In a video that welcomes them into the program, I'll say, "Hey, right now, you're probably overwhelmed. You're probably thinking, *Why the hell did I do this?* You're probably so stressed out. You're on calls, and you have no idea what we're talking about, and you're freaking out. That is normal. You are going to be overwhelmed in the beginning. That's okay. I don't want you to think, *Oh my God, this is so hard. I suck. I don't know any of this stuff.* I want you to change your thought process to, *Oh my gosh, this is awesome. I'm going to learn that. I'm going to know how to do that later.*"

Then I'll tell them, "Oh, and probably about month three or so, there's going to come a time during this training where you're going to be like, 'Why did I ever sign up?' That's normal. When that happens, I want you to remember me telling you that that is normal. Then you push through, because that's going to happen to you. You're on the road to a new path. You're on the road to a new life, a new business. When you're trying to change your business and change your life, it's not always easy. It's hard. Just know that you're going to have those feelings, and when you do, you're going to say to yourself, 'Oh yeah, I'm going to push through. I'm not letting my limited thinking win. I'm going to fight, and I'm going to keep going.'"

You might not know what obstacles they'll run into at first. Take a survey of your people. Ask questions. Ask them what their thoughts are. Nothing is bad or good. How are they thinking, or what do they say to themselves? What obstacles did they come up against? Then, start to teach and train around that.

3. *Create a daily accountability group.* We call ours Skin in the Game. It has been an essential key to the program, and I literally have hundreds of success stories about how helpful it has been and how much it helps people get done and move the needle so much in their business. Also, it helps with community. It's their positive anchor to start their day. Research shows that when you are trying to do a new habit, when you have an anchor of doing something different than before, you're much more likely to sustain and reach that goal. People need some kind of hands-on accountability. (BTW, this is something *every* Million Dollar Coaching program needs! In one-on-one coaching, this accountability is built in. When you build a coaching business that is not one-on-one, you still need to figure out how to give this personal touch.)

I started doing the daily accountability calls called Skin in the Game that I mentioned earlier. A Skin in the Game call is on Zoom, and students show up for 15 minutes each day. They each say one personal commitment and one business commitment. Then, they show up the next day and say whether or not they accomplished their commitments. If they didn't, they say why and how they will overcome that obstacle in the future. Then, they recommit to another (or the same) business and personal goal. (For more training on Skin in the Game, go to Theprovenmodel.com/resources.)

Scan this QR code using the camera app on your phone to access your resource page & added freebies now!

I can't tell you how much Skin in the Game calls have completely helped people with productivity and accountability! With it, students implemented faster, and they were way more successful! Why? Well, for one reason, they didn't want to go to the group to confess they didn't do it *again* the next day. Number two, they were starting off their day with an anchor, something that focused them on their goals.

Early on, I knew this was something that would definitely serve them. I just had to figure out *how* to do it. I didn't have the time to run all these morning calls myself, and I didn't have the money at that point to hire people. But I did have some students who had been with me for a little while who were sharp. They wanted accountability also, and they wanted more access to me. So, I gave them specific training on running these accountability calls and set up a schedule so they handle five calls per week for 15 minutes each day. I check in with them regularly to see how they're doing and give them additional personal attention.

4. *Provide awards and recognition.* I wish I had done this way sooner! ClickFunnels does this better than any company I've ever seen. They have various levels of awards. One is the 2-Comma Plus (shows you've made at least $1 Million using ClickFunnels). People are dying to get one of those. It's the carrot. They want to hang it on their wall, walk on stage, and receive the award. It's a status thing for some to get awards in front of their peers. For some, it validates all their hard work and effort. For me, it's both. Those awards are a walking advertisement for ClickFunnels that cost them nothing because people post their awards all over the internet on various platforms. It's brilliant. It's like free advertising and exposure for the company. Also, it gives people a plan and purpose.

That kind of recognition is very motivational for many people. And it gives other students in the program the thought, *Oh my gosh, if Chris did it, I can do it. If Joanne did it, I can do it.* This is something I wish I had implemented much earlier. It took me about four years to make this part of the program. It's personal marketing and recognition to help motivate people all in one. I recommend that you do this as soon as you can.

5. *Create workbooks for your students.* I've always had workbooks, but not like the workbooks I have now. I used to have PDFs that walked them through, but now I have professionally made workbooks from a company that specializes in them. It shows the journey. It's well thought out. It has gamification and really works with all learning styles to get them the results. It helps them succeed, and it also has all of the awards in it, so they have something to work towards and look forward to. The workbook defines the journey of what they can expect. It builds confidence and reassurance with my students, knowing there is a well thought out journey that will get them to their desired outcome. Mark Stearn of Custom Box Agency is the person who helped me with these. He's amazing and one of the best customer service people I've ever seen (other than me, lol). An addition we made recently was to gamify the program by giving people badges and awards as they do the work in the workbooks and as they hit different achievement levels. People love it. It gives them small goals to work towards.

6. *Make sure you update your content and that it's relevant and current.* Things change, and so should your program. I'm constantly making mine better, and people always notice. Be sure to give them more than you promise. My people are always saying how we over-deliver. They don't want to leave because we keep adding value. Plus, they don't want to leave the community, and some join just for the community. But a great community will only happen if you are picky about who you let in. We have a No Asshole policy, and we live by it. I don't want negative people affecting my community because their negativity spreads like weeds. So, we are careful who we allow in.

7. *Give people a path to ascend.* Is it a one-time program, or are there other levels they can aspire to join? I didn't have that until four years in, and I wish I had thought out the customer journey much sooner. If you don't have higher levels that allow them to stay in, can you create more value and new materials to help with continuity?

Be careful how you do it. Early on, I had something we called Continuity, where people would pay me for the year program, and then we would allow them to stay in the program after the first year at a fraction of the cost. (My program was about $24,000, and we let them stay for $500 per month.) That sounds like a benefit to them, but it wasn't. It was almost like at the back of their mind, they were thinking, *Oh, I can get to that later.* They weren't taking action, and they weren't implementing as quickly and as completely as they should because they figured they had extra time. So, we got rid of the Continuity option. Some of my students were upset at first until they realized that they had been using Continuity as a crutch, as an excuse to procrastinate. Pretty soon, those same people were saying, "Thank you so much, because this gave me the kick in my pants to get started. I don't have time to waste. I've got to do this now." Some people take longer than a year to complete everything, which is fine. They just have to reinvest, and their transformation happens in the transaction. As people pay, they're more likely to actually do what it is that you're telling them to do.

8. Because a lot of my program involves the use of video, *we do their first ten videos for them*, edit them professionally, and walk them through how to feel confident on camera. I added this after four years because we realized how difficult it was for people to do the videos. So, I realized I had to do what it took to help them as much as I could with this early on to help them succeed. This may not be videos for you, but what could it be? What is a big, scary thing people need to do to succeed with your program? Think it through and find out how to support them in getting results.

9. Provide implementation workshops. We want to get people results as quickly as possible, even if it's not monetary. With both my MDMM and real estate coaching, it's typically a while before they see monetary results. It takes time to build the foundation of their business. In order to get them quick wins and see some tangible results, we have workshops where they walk away with the co-author book, marketing plan, funnels, CRM, etc., all completed and ready to go. They get more done in a 4-hour time frame than previously they could in months. This part of the program really helped them, and it helped me with churn.

Take all of these 9 points into consideration as you put your program together, but just start. Don't wait for your program to be perfect! It will evolve as you do. My program worked marvelously when I first started, but it's 1,000% better even now, and it will continue to.

MDMM Mindset: Stop, Snap and Switch

I'm guessing that as you're learning more about the Million Dollar Months Model, you're starting to think, *Hmmm. Maybe I could really do this.* If you're like most people, as soon as you start thinking of the possibility, a lot of fears and negative beliefs pop up. *But I don't have a team. I'm too old to start a business. I don't have the skills…* That's just your fear talking, and you can't let it determine your future.

In my book *Stop, Snap & Switch: Train Your Brain to Unleash Your Limitless Life* (also available in audio), I teach a technique that's really easy and can be used anytime, anywhere. All you need is a rubber band or a hair tie, anything that is easy to take on and off and remove from one wrist to another. I actually had a bunch of elastic wrist bracelets made for myself and my students, but a rubber band works just as well. (If you want one of my special Stop, Snap and Switch bracelets, you can purchase one here: https://www.amazon.com/shop/kristamashorecoaching)

Any time you have *any* type of fear or negative thought in your brain, you stop. That thought can be anything like, *I'm too young. I'm too old. I'm too inexperienced. I'm not good at sales. What if I fail? I don't have enough resources. This is super hard. I'm bad with technology.* It can be any thought about any aspect of your life that isn't positive and constructive. As soon as you catch yourself, that's when you *stop* and acknowledge that you're having a negative thought and that it's not the kind of thought that will get you the life you want.

Next, you *snap* your rubber band or bracelet as soon as you recognize that negative thought. Don't snap the rubber band too hard. You want to feel it, but you don't need to get all black and blue! Next, you *switch* the rubber band to your other wrist, and you rephrase that negative comment into a positive one. If I'm thinking, *Man, I'm too old to go into coaching. No one is going to listen to me.* I'd turn that into, *Hey, my age and experience are going to help me really truly be able to help people.* So, you Stop, Snap and Switch the negative comment into a positive one.

As you keep doing this, you're training your brain to recognize when you're negative and also getting your brain into the habit of restating the negative into positive and shifting your mindset.

CHAPTER 5

The Puzzle Pieces of Ethical Persuasion

I talked about ethical persuasion in the Mindset chapter, but I want to emphasize how very important it is. People are *not* going to get what they want without your help! You have to be really clear about this. **People need to change; they want to change, but they just won't change without your help.** You have to keep making this point during your trainings.

Alan Deutschman wrote a book called *Change or Die*. He wrote that studies of thousands of patients show that 9 out of 10 people who are at risk of heart attack will *not* make the changes they need to take. They're told that they have to stop smoking, eat less and drink less alcohol, avoid lots of stress, and exercise regularly to have the best shot at staying alive. Their doctors told these patients that if they didn't follow through, they would probably *die*. Yet when doctors checked back with them a year later, 9 out of 10 still didn't do it! So, if people who are *facing death* can't make the changes they need to make, what are the odds that your clients will make them?

An insurance company, Mutual of Omaha, got smart and realized that they were paying out a heck of a lot for heart bypass surgeries and angioplasties. In the early 1990s, they hooked up with Dr. Dean Ornish from UCSF to run an experiment. They took 194 patients who had clogged arteries and horrible habits. They gave them the same instructions everybody else got about healthy lifestyle habits, but they added in things like meditation, support groups, aerobics classes, and expert coaches to help them make all the changes in lifestyle they needed to make. They ran this program for one year and then left everyone on their own. *After three years, 77% of the patients were still doing what they needed to do to stay healthy.* They didn't need surgery, and some had even reversed their condition. Two of the most critical keys to this change that probably saved their lives was that they got *coaching* and *support*.

Did you get that? This group, who were told the same thing and had the same information (that they were going to die), were given coaching, accountability, and support so *they were able to make the change that others couldn't*. That's how important it is that you help people and that you sell your services to them because they won't be able to get the help and make the changes if you do not. Keep remembering that *selling is service*. I love selling because I have total conviction that I can help people, *and* I know they need my help to get what they need. Sales is service, and I love it!!

I always talk about GPS and GAS. People have G (goals), but they need a P (plan, blueprint) and an S (strategy) if they want to get where they want to go. Then, if you put GAS (guidance, accountability, and support) in your GPS, it's like putting jet fuel in a plane.

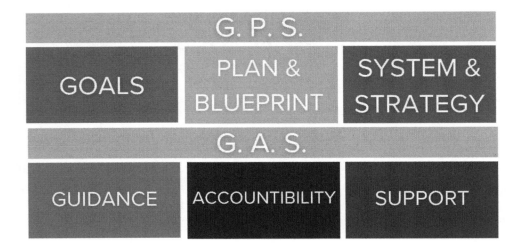

You need to remember this during your trainings and as you learn about ethical persuasion. They are never going to be able to get from point A to point B without our support. ***It's up to us to do anything that we can to help persuade them to sign up for our programs because they need it to get where they want to go.*** Remember, we're not trying to *convince* them. Nobody wants to be convinced. But people do want to be *persuaded* to take action. They just need help saying "yes" to themselves.

They show up to your webinar (or 5-day challenge) or 3-day virtual intensive training because they are *looking for solutions,* or else they wouldn't be there. They feel a gap and a lack in their business or their life in some way or another. That's why they show up. They're looking for help. They're there because they need help. When we've got what they need, and we know it, it is our duty to provide that help to them, to offer them the solution, to give them the guidance and support they need. That's our job.

We have to feel comfortable doing anything and everything we can do to help persuade them to take action. We can't feel like we're *selling* them on something. As I've often said, I believe in sales as service. I love selling because I know that I'm really serving people, adding value, and helping people. It is our job to ethically persuade people in every which way we can to overcome their blocks to saying "yes" to themselves.

Your webinar (or 5-day virtual training) is different from your 2-3 day intensive virtual training. The specific result you're trying to get from the first webinar training and the second intensive training is different, and the points you need to get across are different. That said, they have many of the same components in them that support ethical persuasion. It's like putting together a jigsaw puzzle. You need to have all the right pieces, and you need to put those pieces in the right places. If you drop a couple of pieces of the puzzle on the floor or try to jam pieces in where they don't belong, the whole thing won't come together.

My team and I have spent the past several years finding just the right puzzle pieces, putting them in different arrangements to find out what works and what doesn't. Along with our own experience, I've also studied with some of the best coaches in ethical persuasion and learned techniques from NLP. I've studied coaches and watched trainings just to see how different people persuade and what language they use to get people to take action. I took Myron Golden's training on speaking. I've trained with Eli Wilde, Eli Sanchez, and Suzanne Evans. I even take trainings not related to my own niche to study how they sell. I'm pretty obsessed with it, to be quite frank. So, I know that we've ended up with a formula that is incredibly effective.

Amount I've Spent on My Own Personal Coaching

$224,000 (up until Dec 17, 2020		$6,000	(Copywriting)
$150,00	(Category King)	$9,500	(Speaking)
$150,000	(Atlas)	$15,000	(PR)
$43,000	(Internet Marketing)	$10,000	(Youtube)
$100,000	(Sales)	$12,000	(Ads)
$35,000	(Business Coaching)	$16,000	(AI SEO)
$60,000	(Business Coaching)	$50,000	MEDIA
$$$$	(Mindset)	$30,000	
$$$$	(Personal Development)	$44,000	Eli Wilde (NLP)
$33,000	(Youtube)	$$18,000	Sales
$9,000	(Affiliate Marketing)	$30,000	Leadership
$18,000	(Sales)	$30,000	(Public Speaking)
$2,500	(PR)	$3,600	Mindset Coach
$25K	(Systems)	$15,000	
12K Tik Tok		$30,000	(webinar)
		$$$$$$$$$$$	
		$25,000	

$1,220,200 (5 years and 5 months)

One of my students was invited to speak for 60 minutes at a training, and she was able to make an offer at the end for a program she was selling. She made her offer, and even though she threw in a few of my strategies, she did not sell one thing. Not one person opted in because she was piecemealing the MDMM strategy together. Each and every single thing we do within the MDMM client acquisition and conversion framework has been methodically tested to get the results we are getting. You can't do Million Dollar Months for 31 straight months in a row during a time of recession and uncertainty by piecemealing the model or doing it the wrong way.

All of these pieces have to be built in, and they need to show up in a particular order for each training to get the results you want. Some of these pieces are *techniques,* and some are *specific beliefs or concepts* that you need to instill in your audience. It's all about the timing of it. Seeding the offer, seeding belief in self, seeding belief in the vehicle, and putting in the tactics and strategies that relate to your trainings at the right time in the right sequence. When you do this well and in the right sequence, your audience is already on board with you before you even get to your offer. They are eager and ready to say "yes" to themselves and to you.

All of these techniques and concepts are intended to do 4 key things. We covered them in Chapter One, but they're worth repeating here:

Instill belief in themselves: They need to believe that no matter what their age, skill level, gender, or ethnicity, they can succeed with your program. It doesn't matter if they're starting after failing several times, have a rotten marriage, or never got a college degree; they can be successful. Absolutely everyone has limiting beliefs about themselves. Getting them to believe in themselves is the hardest thing to do and takes the most work. Plus, that self-belief disappears so quickly! You need to help them believe in themselves throughout your trainings and you need to do it so they don't even realize you're doing it. You'll see how we do it using the techniques in this chapter.

Overcome external beliefs: People have all kinds of external reasons (actually, excuses) for why they aren't getting the results they want or why they can't do your program: *I don't have enough time. I can't afford to spend the money. The economy is bad. My high school counselor told me that I wasn't any good at XYZ. My spouse thinks this program won't work for me. My friend told me it's a bad idea.* I'll say more about these external beliefs later. Just keep in mind that limiting beliefs can be both internal and external. Again, *everyone* has some external beliefs that hold them back. People are always looking for ways to prove themselves right about why they can or can't do something and why it won't work for them. If you don't tackle them head-on, these beliefs will undermine everything you're doing.

Instill belief in YOU: The concepts and techniques I'll show you in this chapter are designed to help them gain belief in *you*, your sincerity, and your authenticity. If they don't think you're the real deal, they will not be interested in saying "yes." We've got to get them to believe that you are the authority in what you offer and that there is no one better on this earth to help them. You'll do this by showing them what you've accomplished as well as how you've helped others succeed. You also need to help them see that you are not some kind of superhero, but you started out just like them, and you're relatable and real. You'll do this through sharing personal stories.

Instill belief in the vehicle: They need to believe that *your* program is the one that can help them. They need to know that the program you have put together is unique and effective. You do this in many ways through stories, testimonials, and proof. You have to show off what's unique about your program and how it truly isn't something anyone else is doing. You've got to break down every doubt that can creep up regarding your Big Revelation and any doubts that your program won't work for them. Those doubts will sound like, "I'm not good with technology" or "I've tried something like this before, and it didn't work for me." You've got to show how your program isn't like other things they've tried or done and prove to them why.

Ethical Persuasion Techniques

Seeding for Success

Seeding is just planting different concepts in their heads. These are the ideas you want them to buy into and to have them thinking about before you make your offer. You'll be seeding the value of different parts of your program. You'll be seeding why it's important to learn from others and to get support to achieve their goals. You'll be seeding that they *can* accomplish what they want with the right guidance and that they are worthy of more than what they have now. You'll be seeding the different parts of your offer, as well as belief in themselves, belief in your vehicle, and belief in you throughout the entire presentation, over and over.

I've been relentless about studying people's events, observing their structure and selling patterns, and this is one of the biggest mistakes I've seen most people make. What they lack the most is seeding all of these things. Most people don't do as well or as consistently as they should. I've seen amazing speakers and trainers put on amazing events that you would think would make everyone sign up. But because they didn't continuously seed their offer, seed belief in self, belief in vehicle, and belief in you to help them, they ended up not enrolling as many people as they could, which means they did not help transform as many lives as they could have.

You can plant ideas through stories, examples, testimonials, words of wisdom from others, etc. For example, we have student success panels where our top students share what's working for them. This acts not only as a great teaching tool because the panel shares some great insights, but it also acts to seed belief in my program because they learned so much of what they know through it.

Once you've planted a seed, you can keep referring back to it. For example, to seed the value of my program, I do a whole section comparing McDonald's (which makes $143 Billion per year) to Burger King (which makes $7 Billion per year). I explain in great detail why McD's is different and what differentiates them from Burger King even though they are basically the same kind of company: They both serve fast food, make crappy hamburgers (no offense if you like them!), have French fries and a weird mascot that always comes to mind when you think of them. But what differentiates the two of them are a few things. McDonald's has a clear system for how they do things; they are innovative, they emulate good ideas from other restaurants and make them their own, they have great branding, etc. I teach these principles, and then I relate each of them back to the real estate business. I do this because it shows that you can have two businesses that are virtually the same. But when you compare how they are different in their approach or strategy, you can see how one business will do so much better financially. I want them to see that if they employ these principles, their real estate business can become more successful, too. The principles McDonald's uses are all things that I teach in my program. So, as I give them different strategies related to real estate throughout the training, I'll say, "So, can you see how this would make you like McDonald's, not Burger King?"

To seed the idea of belief in themselves, I've also used the story about the Good Wolf versus the Bad Wolf. The story is told a bunch of different ways, but I say, "A grandmother tells her young grandson that we all have two wolves battling inside of us: the Good Wolf and the Bad Wolf. He then asks, "So which one will win?" and the grandmother says, "The one you feed." I'll then go on to teach them that the Bad Wolf represents fear, self-doubt, and limiting beliefs. The Good Wolf represents confidence, possibility, and courage. Then, throughout the training, I'll stop and say, "So, which wolf are you going to feed? Your fear or your courage?"

Seeding your offer is also so, so important and is woven into the entire presentation like the other things you seed. Everyone needs to know exactly what they are getting, why they need it, and how it is going to transform their lives. You need to touch on these things over and over. Talk about why they need to use the pieces of your offer. For example, in my real estate program, I talk about the co-author book, marketing plan, etc. In my MDMM program, I showcase the funnel we give them that is customized for coaches, the presentation slides for the webinar and 3-day event, the complete sales training we give their sales team, etc. I remind them how they are going to use these things to get the success they want. Show the different ways they can use your materials or tactics in various manners, not just once but multiple times throughout the training. So, by the time you make your Irresistible Life Changing Offer, they know what is in your offer, how they are going to use them, and why they absolutely must have them. They know and feel that all of these things are exactly what they need and why they have not succeeded before.

Once you've planted a seed, refer back to it throughout the training. This is one of the biggest mistakes I see people make. They teach an important point (like the Bad Wolf versus Good Wolf story) but never refer back to it. You need to refer back to those points over and over, and as you teach aspects of your program or high ticket offer, you need to keep referring back to those aspects. Keep showing over and over how what you're offering is going to help them and how they can use it. Most people don't do this very effectively. One of the reasons why we've done so well is that I've nailed this.

The Power of Micro-commitments

This is so important! From the very beginning of your webinar/challenge, you need to get them to make micro-commitments so that when you ask for the big commitments, they're already primed. You ask them for a very small commitment, like keeping their Zoom camera on or staying for an entire 90-

minute session. You ask for a micro-commitment like raising their hand or saying "yes" when they agree with you or writing something in the chat when what you say hits home for them. I have people write on their hands "I'm Next" after they see a great testimonial or success story. I have them write "Do it now!!" when I present a great tactic they can use. Then, I ask them to hold their hands up and show them to the camera. This gets them to *acknowledge* that you and they are on the same team. It moves them over to "your side of the table" rather than sitting across from you, looking skeptical with their arms crossed. Micro-commitments also put people into the natural learning state where they're not just sitting back half listening, but they're participating fully. When they actively participate, they absorb much more of what you're presenting. Study after study shows that people who engage with their bodies and with their voices in answering you will learn more quickly, implement faster, and remember more.

You want to have them say "yes" using different senses. For example, "Can you *see* that if you implement, you can have a different life in 12 months or less? Yes? I can't *hear* you." I say "yes" out loud because I want them to *hear* "yes." "Can you *feel* in your heart that if you actually did the work, put in the time, that you would have a different life?" And I *touch* my own heart as I say this. "Yes, of course you can. Can you *imagine* what your life would be like, how different it would be?" Get their senses involved using *see, hear, touch,* and *feel* along with engaging their *imagination* as they say "yes." Here are some examples of micro-commitments I use that you can tweak to fit your own training:

"I'm going to teach you a ton of great stuff over the next 90 minutes during this webinar. And it really helps me know if you're understanding what I'm saying if I can see you. So, can I get your commitment that you'll turn off your phone, take lots of notes, and keep your camera on? If you'll do that for me, just raise your hand."

"Whenever I teach you a strategy that you know can make you an additional $75,000 from your business, I want you to promise me that you'll write it down in your notebook and put it in the chat. Will you do that? Just raise your hand."

"We all work way too hard to be struggling the way we're struggling. There's got to be a better way, right? Raise your hand if you think so."

"So, even after just three hours, can you see how what I just taught you could substantially improve your business if you implement it? If so, write it in the chat."

"Promise me that before tomorrow, even though what I just taught you is out of your comfort zone, you will implement it. Will you do that for me? For you and your future?"

"Can I ask you a question? Are you open-minded? Good, let's keep being open-minded. When I teach a strategy or a technique, I want you to look for ways that this *will* and *can* work for you. Successful people do that. Unsuccessful people look for reasons why it *won't* work, not why it will. You want to be successful, right? So, let's be open-minded and look for how all the strategies I'm teaching *will* work for you, okay? Can we all do that? Raise your hand and say "yes!"

When you use micro-commitments, you'll have to prompt them, especially at first. "Raise your hand." "Put it in the chat." But after a while, it will start becoming automatic for them. And it may feel awkward for you at first to keep asking them to raise their hands or say "yes." Do it anyway! It really works!

Asking Success Filtering Questions

During your events, you want to get them to prove to themselves the value of what you offer. One of the ways you can do that is through success-filtering questions. I like to use the story of the British national 8-man rowing team in the 2000 Olympics. The team had not won in the Olympics for 88 years! Can you even imagine what 88 years of losing would do to a team's morale? This team knew that if they wanted a different result, they had to do something different every single day. Most people think winning at the Olympics is about what you do in the minutes of the race. But it isn't. It's what you do in all the hours, days, and years leading up to it. And that's what the team focused on changing. How? By asking one question before every big and small decision: "Will this make the boat go faster?"

As one of the team members explained, "Before we'd all get on the rowing machine to practice for 70 minutes, we'd ask, 'Will it make the boat go faster?' Unfortunately, yes. So that's what we'd do. Before going out to the pub, we'd ask, 'Will it make the boat go faster?' Unfortunately, no. So, we didn't." This one question not only kept them focused but gave the men on the team a strong bond, knowing they were all using the same criteria to determine any actions they took. And after 88 years of losing, they won the gold medal in the 2000 Olympics in Sydney, Australia.

After I've told the story, I then use it throughout the virtual event as the success filtering question. After teaching a strategy, I'll say, "So let me ask you. If you implemented just this one idea, would it make the boat go faster?" I'm not *telling* them but *asking* them so the audience can answer for themselves, "Yes, it would."

After every strategy, technique, or mindset training, I ask, "If you do this, would it make the boat go faster? What if you don't implement this strategy? Will it make the boat go faster? Will your business improve or stay where it is at? So, we have to implement this strategy right now. Hard now, or hard forever. Yes, it may cost you time, money, and resources right now to learn this stuff. But you're going to have to pay the price in the short term now, or you're going to pay the price year after year after year after year. Make sense? Put it in the chat. Do It Now!!" By doing this, I am getting them to think it through and come up with the truth. People don't want to spend the money, and they don't want to take the time to get better. But if they don't, they'll be paying the price and losing thousands of hours of time dreaming their dreams rather than living their dreams. By emphasizing this, when it comes to making a decision about enrolling with me, they automatically ask themselves, "Will it make the boat go faster?"

Help Them Persuade Themselves with a Scorecard

We've created a great scorecard that we have people fill in during the event. Basically, anytime we teach something, we ask them to rate themselves on how their business compares. Each of the categories is within our offer that helps them bridge the gap from where they are to where they will go. It shows them all they are missing, and they can see throughout the event how much they lack and how much help they need. It's all about getting them to the realization on their own about what they lack and how much they need our help. (To see one of my scorecards, go to Theprovenmodel.com/resources.)

Scan this QR code using the camera app on your phone to access your resource page & added freebies now!

I'll teach about something that is on the scorecard and ask them to score themselves as to whether they have that in place or not within their own businesses. It keeps them engaged during the event by giving them something to do. It also keeps their brain in the realization of, "Wow, I am really bad in this area. I need help." Typically, 90% of the things mentioned on the scorecard are things they are not doing or don't have in place. Every time I ask them to score themselves, they see how much they are lacking in their current business. The scorecard is important because they are rating themselves and all of the areas of weakness without me pointing it out to them. The scorecard includes everything that I am offering and have taught them about over the past three days.

This is also effective because when they get on the phone with my sales team, my sales team asks them to pull out their scorecards. "So, tell me, what are the biggest areas of weakness you see in your business?" Usually, it's everything! But again, it's not my salesperson saying that. They are saying it themselves. ***The more they tell us what they need instead of us telling them, the more they will convert and say "yes" to themselves, which ultimately is "yes" to us as well.***

The Science of Successful Modeling

You have to model what you're teaching throughout the event. You can't encourage them to be confident if everything in your body language says that you don't believe what you're presenting. You can't tell them to put energy into their business or marriage or health if you look half asleep and you're ready for a nap. You can't convince them that it's okay if they're not perfect if you aren't willing to make mistakes in front of them and admit it. You can't encourage them to be authentic or unique if you won't let them see who you really are.

You need to model what you teach. A psychology professor from UCLA, Dr. Albert Mehrabian, researched body language. He said that communication happens 55% nonverbally, 38% vocally, and only 7% through words. Even though *information* is communicated through words, he found that ***your body language, energy, and facial expressions have a huge impact on how people interpret that information, whether they believe you and whether they like you.***

I am like the Energizer Bunny on steroids, and I always have been. When I get in front of an audience, I get even more energized. In fact, I have to work to slow myself down because I get talking so fast that no one can understand me! When I teach for two hours, I feel like I've physically worked out for two hours!

All of the successful trainers I've seen have high energy. You don't have to be exactly like me, but you do have to kick your energy up a notch while you're doing these trainings. First of all, it helps people stay awake and pay attention. If you look bored and drone on and on, you'll just put them to sleep. Also, success in anything requires high energy. Remember, high energy equals high income. The more energy you have during the presentation, the more money and impact you will make. And it relates to your clients as well in both their business and personal life. If they want a happier relationship, they'll have to put more energy into it. If they want to make more money, they'll have to put more energy into it. If they want to be healthier, they'll have to put more energy into it. Model that high energy for them. I have a saying, and I repeat and model it throughout my trainings: "It's a Universal Law that High Energy = High Income."

Identity Shaping: The Secret Ingredient

You want people at your trainings to start identifying as successful people who can do what it takes to get what they want. They may not have thought of themselves that way before. I start from the very beginning by saying, "Just the fact that you showed up today and committed your precious time to learn something new means that you're in the top tier of real estate agents out there." I incorporate a lot of NLP in my training now, saying things like "successful people know…" or "really smart people know…" It subtly tells them that I'm talking to a very smart person—them! Or I'll say things like, "A coach has a coach. My coach's coach has a coach because *successful people know* how important it is to have a coach." I say this because I want them to emulate and associate success with having a coach. All of this language is woven throughout my presentations.

I'll present the idea of being a Doer who implements rather than a Dabbler who just learns something and then doesn't apply it. Then, throughout the event, I'll remind them, "We're Doers, not Dabblers, right?" And I do this because I want them to associate their identity as being a person who Does, not someone who just Dabbles. We all identify as "certain kinds of people," and our identities (both negative and positive) can be really powerful in impacting what we do and how we feel. I want them to start identifying in a positive way.

I had an encounter with Tony Robbins recently. It was one of the most amazing experiences of my life. I have dealt with an issue for many years. Tony worked with me personally for 70 minutes in front of 9 other individuals. (We had all won a challenge, and part of the prize was this intimate setting with Tony.) He said, "Krista, you have to change your identity. You've been dealing with this because you're identifying yourself as this being a part of you. Until you change your identity, you'll struggle with this." It hit me like a rock. I said to myself, "I have been identifying myself with this problem." This encounter will stick with me forever as I'm trying to improve who I am.

Leveraging Testimonials for Trust and Belief

Testimonials can make a huge impact. They are "social proof" where the audience gets to see that it's not just you who can succeed based on what you're offering, but others can succeed with it as well. The key is to use your testimonials correctly.

First of all, you need to use many different types of testimonials, some video and some text, different ages, races, genders, and ethnicities, and different levels of experience in what you're teaching. You want to make sure there's enough variety in your testimonials that everyone can find some that they really relate to. This helps instill one of the key beliefs they need: Belief in themselves. They see that a variety of people have succeeded who are no smarter or more experienced and who are about their same age, sex, and ethnicity, and that helps them believe in themselves.

I tell people that when they see a success story, they imagine themselves having that same success. Some people in the past have said I have too many testimonials. Once I started telling them to see themselves having that success, we now get fewer complaints. And now the group will defend me if someone complains. In the chat, they'll say, "She's doing that because she wants us to see ourselves in these success stories." This is an example of what I mean when I say that each and every aspect of the event is set up precisely because we've experienced someone or something that has been an issue or that has shown up as an obstacle for participants. Once we identify it, we respond to it. We modify the trainings over and over whenever we discover something that will help it be more effective.

Also, you want your testimonials to feature different parts of your program and the *specific* results students got from those parts. This helps instill another key belief: Belief in your vehicle. This is part of the seeding process that I talked about above. You're seeding within them the value of each part of your program because, in the testimonial, they can see how much that specific part helped one of your students, which means it can help them, too.

The main point to get across with testimonials is that "If they can do it, so can you." In fact, I tell the people in my trainings, "Every time you see a testimonial from one of my students or I tell you about a success I've had, I want you to say out loud, 'If they can do it, so can I!'" I tell them to write "I'm next!" on their hand and hold their hand up and say, "I'm next!" Getting people to believe in themselves and that they can succeed is the *most important* and the *hardest* thing to do. People lose belief very quickly. It's actually very sad.

I like to tell the story about one of my mentors, Brent Gove. He is the sweetest guy, and he makes around $1 Million a month (give or take) *residually* because he's grown a huge organization as part of eXp (a real estate company). When I see his results and success, even though he's been in it so much longer than me, I say to myself, *If Brent can do it, so can I.* That helps me take massive action, have a great attitude, and believe that I can actually accomplish it. The alternative would be thinking that his level of success is far out of my reach or I don't have the skill set or know enough people. Which one do you think will serve me better? Thinking I can or thinking I can't? Which one would serve your clients better?

What if you're just starting out and don't have any students yet? When I started my real estate coaching program, I had mentored a few people but never set up a whole training course. So, I found around 40 people and gave my new course to them for free. Then I coached them and helped them so they achieved a level of success. That gave me some of my first testimonials. This also helped me with my own belief that my program would work. Remember, he who has the most conviction wins the debate. I needed to be convinced with 100% certainty that I could actually help people. Coaching these first students for free and seeing their success helped build my conviction and belief, which helped me ethically persuade others so that I could serve them!

As soon as I launched my program, I actually started having people give me testimonials during the virtual event itself. They'd talk about how much they had already learned from me. I always tell people, "You don't get what you want. You get who you are. So, if you want people to do things for you, you have to be willing to do things for people." During my training, I teach them how important good reviews are for their business, and I'll teach them how to request reviews. I show them how my software, the Mashore Method, can give them the traction on their reviews very, very quickly by sending out a mass text message, sending out an email, and automatically putting those reviews on Google and directly on different digital platforms. After I teach them the concept, I'll say, "Okay, now I'm showing you this.

Can you do it for me? Remember, if you want to get reviews from people, you have to be willing to give them. So, how many of you are willing to give me a review right now? Remember "5 stars" only. Awesome. Go do it right now. We're going to take a five-minute break." I end up with over one hundred reviews within those few minutes.

At the beginning especially, I would also utilize examples from other industries. For example, the co-author book was part of my offer, so I had people who could talk about how important being an author is, how it gives you authority in the market, and how much it helps grow your reputation and business. I would show the book of a photographer I know and show her video testimonial where she says, "Being an author in my field has been one of the biggest things I've used to fast track my business." Then I'll say, "If writing a book on being a photographer has helped fast-track her business, imagine how it would help you to be an author in the real estate industry. It would position you as an authority and a cut above your competition."

Understanding Price Marinades

When you marinate meat, basically, what you're doing is adding flavor and tenderizing the meat before it's cooked. Rather than just tossing it on the grill and throwing a bunch of spices on it, you're giving the flavorings time to settle in. A price marinade is the same thing. You're letting people soak in the idea of how much your program is worth throughout the event, so by the time you get to the actual offer and price, they're already comfortable with it. One thing, though: The price you use for marinating is *much* higher, usually three times what your actual price is.

For example, as I start the trainings for my real estate coaching business, I write $75,000 on the whiteboard and say, "Okay, every time you hear an idea or see something that, if you implement it, it could generate another $75,000 in your business, write it down in your notebook. Then put in the chat, "$75k idea!" I leave the $75,000 on the whiteboard, or somewhere they can see it the entire time. And throughout the training, I'll say, "Okay, so if you implemented this one thing I just taught you, do you think you could generate another $75,000 in your business? If so, write it down." Hands go up, they write it in the chat, and they get all excited. I'm marinating the value of a $75,000 offer.

But then, when I get to the offer, the offer is only $25,000, and I say to them, "Okay, look back at your notebook, all the $75,000 ideas you've had in the short time we've had together. Count them up. Do you have at least 10? So, you're saying that if you do all those things, that's $750,000 worth of ideas that I gave you to implement your business? So, I could charge you $75,000 for this program because, according to what you just said, it would be worth much more to you than that. But guess what? It's only $25,000." You price marinate a higher price the entire time, and they're getting comfortable with it. And they are *proving to themselves* how much value they could get out of it.

How would this work if your coaching is not about business or making more money? Say, for example, your program is for women who are suffering from menopause, and that the price of your program is $5,000. If you just threw out this price without marinating it, it might seem really high. But what if you use the price marinade of $15,000? Menopause usually lasts around seven years, but it can take as long as 14! Women are desperate to get relief from its symptoms, especially when they understand that those symptoms aren't going away anytime soon!

So, during the training, as you show them how they could get rid of mood swings, night sweats, sleepless nights, and depression, you could say, "Would it be worth $15,000 to you to not feel like a crazy person, have sleepless nights or be depressed over the next 7 to 14 years?" You teach them how to get their energy back. "How much would it affect your career, your business, or your family if you had your energy back over the next 7 to 14 years? Would it be worth $15,000?" You show them how they could enjoy sex again. "Would it be worth $15,000 to enjoy sex with your husband or partner again for the next 7 to 14 years and beyond?" You teach them how to get rid of the night sweats. "What if you didn't have to wake up every night in soggy sheets and pajamas from the night sweats for the next 7 to 14 years? Would that be worth $15,000?" Honestly, as a woman who can relate to all of this, getting my life back this way would be *priceless*! But even though you can't really put an exact price on these things, you want to come up with a specific number to marinate, not just "priceless." They need to get a definite figure in their minds.

The Impact of Data-Driven Narratives

There's an old saying that "Statistics tell, and stories sell." You need both. Statistics are important for the left side of the brain (which is logical and analytical) to make it feel comfortable that what you're saying is accurate and true. Some people in your audience will be more analytical than others, but everyone likes to see a statement backed up by quantifiable facts. As often as you can, bring in statistics that confirm a point you're making. It will make your point much more impactful. Think about it: Is it more persuasive to hear that "The Pomodoro technique really helps with productivity" or "87% of my students were able to complete their five weekly videos in less than one hour using the Pomodoro technique." How about the difference between "Most coaches do not make a lot of money at what they do" versus "The average business coach in California makes $97,753, and the range falls between $82,406 and $119,208." The one with specific numbers hits home and feels more true, right?

This brings up an important point about statistics: Whether it's numbers you've gathered from your own experience or that you've gotten from someplace else, do *not* use rounded-off numbers like "50%" or "90%." They just aren't as believable as "49.7%" or "91%." People tend to round off and use numbers like 25%, 50%, 75%. My brain automatically goes, *That number can't be right. How is it that all of them are perfect?* It's a little like when you buy something at the grocery store, and it turns out to be exactly

$33.00 or $155.00. It seems unreal to us somehow. So, be as specific as you can about the numbers. Do not round up (round down if necessary). It is most likely more accurate and more believable to the brain.

Crafting Captivating Stories

Unlike statistics, stories relate more to the left side of the brain, the part of the brain that deals with creativity, intuition, and feeling. It turns out that our brains are wired for stories. We've been telling stories to each other since we lived in caves and just grunted at each other! When we hear a good story, our bodies release more oxytocin, the "feel-good hormone." Also, now that researchers can actually look into the brain, they can see that we have *five times more* neural activity in our brain when we hear a good story. Our brains literally light up as the neurons fire more electrical impulses. Neuroscientists claim that "neurons that fire together, wire together." So, when you hear or read a good story, your brain's neurons wire together. This causes you to remember much more of the information than if you just got it in a boring lecture.

Stories can be powerful teachers and persuaders, but they have to be *good* stories! You know those long, boring stories that someone tells you about their latest visit to the dentist or the weird dream they had last night? My husband does this. He has the weirdest dreams that go on and on. Although I love hearing him and listening to him, when it comes to his crazy long, make-no-sense, drawn-out dreams, I tend to wander off (sorry, love!).

That's not the kind of story you need. You need to tell engaging and entertaining stories that make a clear point, whether they're stories from your own experience or stories about someone else. Your stories have to be relatable so your audience can imagine themselves in the shoes of the story's hero. When you tell stories, you bring them into it. Say things like, "Has that ever happened to you?" "Do you remember something similar?" "We all have issues, don't we?" You also need to paint a picture so that your audience can *feel* what you're talking about, even if they've never directly experienced it themselves. Your story needs to be *compelling* so that your audience is really eager to hear the outcome. And they need to envision themselves in the story. They need to be able to relate it to themselves so they can see how they can improve or get better, too.

You'll use stories to illustrate points and teach certain concepts. But one of the most powerful ways you'll use it is to tell part of your own history so that people can relate to you. They need to see you as human to solidify that belief of, "If she can do it, so can I."

When I'm teaching about the importance of finding a compelling why to keep you motivated to take action, I use the story of my divorce (Chapter 1) when I was left with virtually no money in the bank. I desperately wanted to give my two little girls a good, happy home and security. I was in survival mode. It was the motivation, the why, that built my business and put me in the top 1% of all Realtors® in the nation.

So, when I tell this story during an event, what does it do? First of all, it makes me relatable. It shows that I had to overcome some tough times, and if I can do it, so can they. It also relates to the importance of finding your why as motivation for success. It's a personal story that makes a lot of points, and because it's so personal, they'll remember it.

Celebrating Wins for Momentum

This is another really great technique: You want your audience to experience some kind of small wins for themselves during the event based on what you're teaching them. And most importantly, you want them to announce their wins to encourage others to do the same and so you can celebrate with them. For example, in my real estate webinar, I'll teach them how to do video text messages as a marketing tactic. Then, during the lunch break, I have them do five short video texts to old clients just saying "Hi. I've been thinking about you and hope you're doing well." That's it. When they come back after the break, they report what they did in the chat. That's their first win! Even though they were nervous, they did it anyway! We celebrate that like crazy as their first step to creating the business they really want. Then (because the video calls really *can* get fast results), we almost always have one or two people who got great leads or even listings from their lunch break video text! They put it in the chat, and we celebrate those wins as well.

These quick wins *prove* to people in real-time that what you're teaching really works—and can work for them. It immediately builds trust in you and your program. And it plants the seed of "Hey, if I could get a win with just one small thing she taught me, how much farther could her coaching get me?"

In your trainings, you want to make sure you have some sort of activity as often as you can. What can you create that gives them quick wins that they can feel successful at? This is important because it's showing them, "Wow, if she can help me during this short time frame, what would it be like if I actually worked with her for a year?" You also need to relate back to this win when you make your Irresistible Life Changing Offer. "Remember when you did the video text message and the positive results you got from that? And that was from a $47 investment on Day 1. Imagine if we get the opportunity to work together and you invest in your success and results. Imagine what else I'll be able to do for you and how I'll be able to help you." Remember, all of these things put together help us get Million Dollar Months and give us the opportunity to change lives and help people.

Delivering Value-Packed Content

Maybe this is obvious to you, but since you're positioning your webinar and 2-3 day event as *trainings,* they really need to have some meat to them. If your coaching program is about parenting skills, you need to give them specific tactics and insights into parenting. If your program is about helping people create businesses from home, you need to give them specific tools and ideas that will help them do that. At the end of the day, whether they sign up with you or not, you want everyone who attends to walk away feeling like their time was really well spent. You want them to feel like you already gave them something that will improve their lives in some way.

I saw an analogy from a newsletter by Pat Flynn. He said, "… I don't want to be the house handing out candy at Halloween, only to be forgotten about at a moment's notice. I want to be the chef at a restaurant that people want to dine at and not only be satisfied but come back again with some friends, too." That's what valuable content needs to be. Something that makes such an impact that people want to hear more and want to tell others about it. You want them to want to come back for more or, even better, invest in themselves for an extended period of time to get the results that they want faster and more efficiently within your program.

Personally, I was always the one who wanted to be the house all the kids remembered on Halloween. Year after year, I would buy the *large* candy bars, even the *Jumbo* ones, and hand them out. Maybe I just felt inadequate and wanted to be liked. Maybe it was because I was raised a Jehovah's Witness (though I am no longer), and we were not allowed to Trick or Treat. Whatever the reason was, I definitely made an impact when I went over the top on Halloween :o).

Alex Hormozi said something in one of his books that really hit home with me. "If you're not giving enough of your good stuff away, you're not giving away enough." And he also says, "If you're not a little afraid about what you're giving away, you're not giving away enough." You might be afraid that you're giving too much meat and people will come to your trainings and then go off and try to do it on their own. People will go off and try it on their own, but most likely, they weren't your ideal Client anyway. In my experience, that isn't a problem. I give as much good stuff away in my books and free trainings and I still make millions of dollars each month because people need my help to piece it all together— and they need your help, too!

Serve, don't sell.

It might be tempting to get right to your "sales pitch" (Irresistible Life Changing Offer), but the greatest "pitch" in the world won't move them to action if they don't know that you have their best interests at heart and that you have tons of valuable knowledge. You're not going to teach them everything in your entire program even if you could during these trainings. (It's impossible to do that in 3 days). And remember, the goal isn't to teach—it's to transform. That's also why the mindset portion of the trainings is so important.

A mentor once told me, "Krista, you teach too much. You can't transform someone's life in a 90-minute webinar or a 3-day event. That's not the goal. The goal is to move them enough through your stories, etc., to get them to believe that this will work for them." That's why this framework works so well. It's all perfectly positioned to get them to say "yes" to themselves. That said, be generous with what you know. Give them more than they thought they'd get. It's better to give them too much rather than too little.

Ethical Persuasion Concepts

Using these techniques (stories, seeding, testimonials, etc.), you'll be planting certain concepts and ideas throughout the trainings. When people understand and buy into these concepts, they are much more likely to say "yes" to themselves and "yes" to you.

Brain and Beliefs

I spend a ton of time on how the brain works and the importance of beliefs during the trainings because it is the foundation of everything they need to understand. They will need this foundation to succeed at whatever you are teaching them. They need to have this foundation so they can see that they *can change* and *can change their lives for the better.*

You need to teach them about how the brain works and how beliefs get wired into them. You need to show them that their beliefs are not necessarily true and that it's their beliefs that run everything in their lives. They need to really understand that where they are in life, in their business, their relationships, and even their health are all based on their beliefs.

When they understand the brain and beliefs, it's like a bowling ball. When you throw a bowling ball down the lane, you can knock down all the pins at the end or pick off one or two. Without that ball, though, how can you knock any pins down? Blow them over like blowing out birthday candles? Run down the lane and kick them over? No! You need the bowling ball.

Teaching them about the brain and beliefs is your bowling ball. ***They truly need to get that their beliefs are not the truth, and these beliefs have brought them to where they are, and that they have the power to retrain their brains to get different results in their lives.*** When they understand this, they become open to the other new ideas you're presenting. Without it, you'll run into resistance with every idea you try to get across.

I can't get into everything you need to know about the brain and beliefs here. If you don't already have a good understanding of how the brain works and the power of beliefs, I'd highly recommend you pick up my book *Stop, Snap & Switch: Train Your Brain to Unleash Your Limitless Life* (there's an audio version as well). In there, you'll find some analogies, stories, and studies I've used myself to teach it.

Fear

This is really part of how the brain works, but it's such a big issue for most people that I wanted to make sure you deal with it. ***Fear is the number one thing that makes people do or not do something.*** It has to do with the amygdala and the way we've been wired since caveman times. Fear is what keeps people from starting new businesses, asking people out on dates, trying new strategies, and being vulnerable in communication with their partners. And fear, especially fear of change, is what will keep them from joining your program.

I recently worked with this awesome, very successful, guys' guy type of man. You would think he had no fear whatsoever. But he did. He's a great salesperson and has a huge audience with millions and millions of followers. I kept telling him that people would easily pay $50k just to be in a mastermind with him. He kept saying, "I don't see what the value is. I can't sell it if I don't see the value in it." I kept saying, "You don't get it. Just by being in the room with you, they'll get the value. They will see more of what's possible. You lead by example."

I Am Not a Unicorn

People need to know that you are *not* some superhuman being and that you're just like them. Look, I'm not exceptional. I'm the kid who was a bedwetter who had a central processing disorder and couldn't really read until I was in the 4th grade, who ended up in juvenile hall. I was abused as a kid and started out with all sorts of beliefs that I wasn't good enough, smart enough, or lovable enough. I had to work really hard to change those beliefs and get where I am today. And I still have to work on them. In the beginning, with each of my businesses, I had absolutely no clue what I was doing. I had to put a lot of time, energy, resources, and money into figuring out each different business.

But people look at me and think, *Well, obviously **she** could do it because she's so positive and confident* (years of therapy and work on myself). *She's so cute with that blond hair* (hair extensions), *pretty white teeth* (veneers that fall out all the time), *and great shoes* ($39 from DSW). *Plus, she's so smart* (I'm the kid who couldn't read until 4th grade) *and knowledgeable* (I've spent thousands of hours and literally $1,220,200 in just over six years in trainings). They don't see where I came from.

That's why sharing your personal story is so important. Your story may not be as tough as mine, but it doesn't matter. We've all had ups and downs and things we've had to overcome. Let them see that you are just a person who has dreams and goals like them. Let them see that you didn't start out perfect, and you aren't perfect now. When I screw up during a training, I point it out. "If I can mess up like that and still have the success I have, you can too. None of us has to be perfect."

Investment versus Liability

When people spend money, they tend to focus on the *cost*. When *successful* people spend money, they focus on the *value*. And successful people also recognize the difference between paying for something that is just a liability and something that is an investment, whereas many of the people showing up to your trainings don't know the difference. Successful people who are comfortable with money don't look at what things are going to cost. They look at the *value* that will come out of the investment. People who don't have a good relationship with money (which is probably 95% of all people!) look at what things are going to cost and don't look at the value of things. You need to help people focus on the *value* that will come out of the investment with you.

Warren Buffet has often said that the best investment you can make is in yourself. With an investment, you expect to get a return on it. You'll either get an increased financial return, or you'll get something that will increase the quality of your life. On the other hand, a liability is when you're paying for something like a car, a movie, or dinner out. The car may be sexy, and the dinner and movie might be fun, but are they really an investment? No. You may enjoy those things, but they don't give you a financial return or really increase the quality of your life, right? Enrolling in your program is an *investment*, not a liability, and they need to understand that. It's an investment because it's increasing their skill set. It's adding to their resources to make them a better person or to help them create a more successful business. The one thing no one can take away from you, no matter what the economy does or what life throws at you, is the investment you make in your own skill set and knowledge to make your life or business better. You'll always have that. The car, vacation or any material things are liabilities that can be taken away. But the investment in yourself and your business can never be taken from you.

Beliefs About Money

We've all got tons of limiting beliefs, but one of the biggest areas is about money. People also have a lot of crazy ideas about money. It's SO common! They think they aren't worthy enough to make a lot of money or that if they make a lot of money, their friends won't like them (get new friends!). They think making money is hard and that they'd have to give up everything else to make it. They think that people with lots of money must take advantage of others or be mean in some way. You probably have some of those crazy ideas yourself! So, especially if your program involves helping people make more money, you really need to tackle these beliefs up front. Why? Because even if they *say* they want more money, limiting beliefs about money will keep them from doing the very thing they need to do to have more money.

Believe me, I've had to work on my own beliefs about money. I haven't lived at home since I was 13. I was sent on my own once I graduated from high school and literally had to fend for myself for anything and everything. Then my first husband left me with two little ones and zero in the bank—trust me, I've had to work and work and work on my relationship with money. Now, I'm a multi-millionaire, and money isn't an issue. But it wouldn't have happened if I had not made overcoming limiting beliefs a priority, recognized I had issues, took extreme ownership of those issues, and then was relentless in my pursuit to change them. I would *not* be where I am in most areas of my life.

If your program isn't about making more money, there is probably a core belief around your topic that is similar. For example, for people wanting to improve their marriage, some crazy core beliefs might be *Real people don't live happily ever after.* Or *I don't deserve to be that happy.* Or *Marriage is supposed to be easy. It must be wrong if it's hard.* If your program is helping people write their autobiographies, crazy core beliefs might be, *I don't know how to write.* Or *No one would be interested in what I have to say.* Or *People might think less of me when they know my story.* Whether these common, crazy core beliefs are money or something else, you need to tackle them and get them out of the way.

I've had to tackle different issues and core beliefs several times in my own life. I had to look at the way I was leading my team and make changes. I had to take extreme ownership surrounding issues in my marriage and work on that. I've had to face limiting beliefs about my children. I've had issues around food. You name it, I (and probably you too) have had to and will continue to be honest with myself about the changes I need to make and serious about doing the things I need to do to make those changes. It's a relentless pursuit of growth and working towards being the best version of myself. You and your clients will need to do that, too.

Nightmare and Dream

We're all driven by the carrot and/or the stick, by pleasure and/or pain. People tend to be more driven by pain. If you've dived deep into your Ideal Client, you should know what their nightmares and their dreams are. During your trainings, it's super important to help them really *feel* them. You want them to truly *feel* what it would be like if they could get what they want in life. Then, you want to remind them over and over that their dream is possible. You also want them to stay aware of their nightmare. That if they don't take action to change, this nightmare could actually become reality. This is really important, getting people to see the *cost* of inaction. **People are more likely to buy when they realize the huge cost of not doing anything.** You've literally got to get them to feel the pain. Pain is more motivating than pleasure.

People *know* what their dreams and nightmares are, and they think or worry about them. But sometimes, they don't get into *feeling* them enough to get motivated to take action. Your job is to bring their dreams and nightmares forward. You need to help them experience, "Wow! If I had my dream business/marriage/body, this is how great it would feel! These are all the things I could do or have! This is what it would mean for the rest of my life!" Then, because people are often more driven by nightmares than dreams, you need to help them experience the opposite. "If I don't change anything, where will I be a year from now? Five or ten years from now? How will that affect the rest of my life? Even more so, how will it affect my family and kids?" You need to ask them, "How long has this been happening? What if it continues to happen?" It has to become real for them, not just a vague worry.

MDMM Mindset: Momentum

One thing successful people have in common is they've developed the *skill of momentum*. They weren't born with it, but they learned it and are really good at using it when they find themselves dragging their feet. They know exactly what they need to do: Reconnect to their compelling why and vision and strengthen their certainty that they can achieve what they've set out to do. You can learn to use this skill, too, by *visualizing success in your mind in advance* and constantly reconnecting to your vision and your why. You've got to keep that fire lit in your belly, and you've got to rewire your neural pathways so that your sense of certainty runs automatically through your whole body. It's not enough to do this once. You need to devote time *daily* to visualizing your MDMM business and all the good it will bring to you and others until it is so clear and experiential that you have no doubt that you'll achieve what you want.

CHAPTER 6

Your Irresistible Life Changing Offer

Now that you know your Ideal Client, have information on your competitors, and you've discovered your Big Revelation, you're ready to put together an Irresistible Life Changing Offer! Yes, your offer has to be so good that they can't wait to say "yes" to you! Your offer has to be so good that they have absolutely no doubt that it is worth every penny you're charging! Your offer has to be so good that they know *exactly what it is and* what they need to get what they want and where they want to go! They know exactly how it is going to save them time, make them money, or get them the exact result that they are looking for.

But before we go any further in creating your Irresistible Offer, let me pass on a warning. You have to be *extremely* careful about promising clients and students that they will get specific results, especially when it comes to money. The Federal Trade Commission (FTC) has gone after training programs that promise people that they'll make tons of money. I'm guessing that the American Psychiatric Association (APA) would come down hard on coaches who promise to cure mental or emotional illnesses. Your offer can still be irresistible without crossing these lines.

Besides, you can never promise results because coaching and training is a "do with" process, not a "do for" service. You can give them the best training in the world, mountains of terrific materials, and all the support they could ever need. But if they don't do the work, they won't get the results. Period. You can certainly show them the results that you or your students have gotten by applying what you teach. But you have to make sure they understand that results will vary from person to person. Some people will progress faster than others. Some people will hit 100% of their goals, and others will hit 75% or 50%. (From what I've seen, this has more to do with the effort, energy, mindset, and resources they're willing to give to the work rather than anyone being smarter or more talented.) You have no control over what they do, so don't put yourself in a bad situation by promising results you can't control. Also, I'm not a lawyer, so be sure to talk to your attorney about using success stories, case studies, or testimonials anytime there is any sort of income claim. For example, a student might say, "I made $25,000 in a month." Well, even though that is a true statement, unless that is the typical and the norm, you still need to be careful. It would be better to have them say, "I sold five products at $5,000 each."

Personally, I *know* that *anyone* who works at it and applies what I teach them will get the results they're after. But I don't guarantee it because I can't control what they will do. When I first started out, I tried giving a guarantee. "If you do the work for three months and get no results, we'll refund 100% of what you paid." It was a hot mess! People went ahead and downloaded all the materials, then came looking for a refund. People who hadn't done a thing for three months demanded a refund. It only happened with a few people, but it was still frustrating to deal with. We knew that they hadn't stuck by their side of the bargain, but if we didn't refund their money, we knew they'd bad-mouth the program. (Some went ahead and badmouthed the program even after we gave them their money back!) So, we rewrote our contract and now don't give any guarantees. We make it clear that we'll provide what we said we would, and it's up to them to do the work.

I tell people enrolled in my program, "Hey, you invested in yourself and in me to help you. If I just let you out of your contract, then I'd be letting you down as your coach. You committed to this, and you've got to see it through. You're not going to get the results by giving up on yourself. If I let you out, I'm giving up on you. So, get to work and start implementing, and you'll see the results you wanted to get when you signed up."

However, there is a lot of evidence that when you give some sort of guarantee, your sales will go up. You can give a guarantee if they do certain things and can *prove* that they did the work, then you will give them a refund. For example, for my program, I'd want them to show me that they went through all the trainings, did the worksheets, showed up to all of my calls, went to Skin in the Game 85% of the time, met with their accountability coach each week, and did their daily sheet each day. If they still don't get any results after that and they can prove they did all the things, then I'd give them their money back. I could do this because, literally, if they do all that stuff, in my humble opinion, it would be impossible for them not to get results!

I do, however, give a guarantee about my 3-day event when I present it in the webinar. I say, "I am so confident that you'll get so much value out of the 3-day event that on the first day, if you don't think you've gotten the value of what you paid for the three days, I'll give you a full refund. So, you have nothing to lose, and there is no risk, so go sign up right now, and I'll see you on Monday."

Creating Your Irresistible Life Changing Offer

In my MDMM program, we help students create their Irresistible Offer during our Value Creation Workshop. (I learned the term "Irresistible Offer" from Alex Hormozi, who wrote the book *100 Million Dollar Offers*. He's an incredible marketer and taught me a lot.) We run students through several exercises and have them answer a number of questions. Then we test their Irresistible Life Changing Offer in front of my team and other students to make sure it really is so great that their Ideal Client will be eager and enthusiastic about saying "yes." If it isn't, we help them tweak it until the offer is outstanding.

I can't emphasize enough how important your offer is. I also took a training from Jason Fladlein at his Driven Mastermind, and he said he would spend literally days and days going over the offer to make it almost impossible to say "no." Many times, the bonuses alone are worth more than the actual offer. In fact, Jason talked about how Alex Hormozi hired him to help Alex create an irresistible offer. Alex worked on it with his team for 4-5 days prior to meeting with Jason. Then he and Jason worked for 3-4 very long days, making the offer even better. Then, once he left Jason, Alex and his team spent another 20-30 hours on it! That's how important your offer is.

To put your offer together, don't just start by thinking about what you've always taught and the materials you created that you already have on hand. Instead, begin the process by thinking back to your Ideal Client. I heard Jason Fladlien say once, "You'll sell them what they want, but you'll *give them what they need*." What he meant was that your Ideal Client may *want* a flourishing yoga studio, but what they *need* is to become better at marketing. They may *want* a fulfilling marriage, but what they *need* are better communication skills. What they may *want* is to have a well-trained dog, but what they *need* is to become a better dog owner. Throughout all of the Million Dollar Month Model, you'll be learning to connect what they *want* to what they really *need*. Your Irresistible Offer is based on what they really *need* to get what they *want*.

To help you get there, try answering these questions. Since I did this myself recently before I first started coaching people on the Million Dollar Month Model, I'll use my own MDMM offer as the example. As I do this, I want you to be thinking about your own business.

What are the dream outcomes for your Ideal Client? You should already have a good idea of your Ideal Client's dream, but get specific. For the coaches and people who have high ticket offers who are my Ideal Clients, they want to train and coach hundreds or maybe even thousands of people. They are committed to creating a quality program that gets results for their clients and students. They want to take their business to the next level in all areas—systems, marketing, profitability, reach, lead generation, lead nurture, conversion, fulfillment, and delivery. They want to have a sustainable, large income month after month. They may aspire to the Million Dollar Month level, or they may just want to be at the six-figure level, but they want to make substantially more than most coaches. Most coaches really want to help people; they want to get their clients the results they desire. They want to help better their clients' lives. They need to figure out how to get people to be more productive, to be held more accountable, and how to get them to say "yes" to themselves. My Ideal Client wants to figure out how to do all of this without constantly working crazy hours and ruining their own quality of life. They may even want to figure out how to structure their business so that it keeps producing even if they were to take a three-week vacation or need time to focus on creating a new business.

My Ideal Client also wants to be profitable. They're stuck at seven figures a year. And the old tactics that got them to 7-figure *years* won't get them to 7-figure *months* or eight figures annually in their business. They are tired of all the shiny objects. They've paid too many coaches who promised the world but fell short. They just want a clear path with step-by-step instructions from someone they trust who has actually accomplished what they are trying to accomplish.

Now, ask yourself that same question and write down your answers. Next, write down all the specific ways that you can help them get what they want.

What do they see as obstacles or problems to getting what they want? This is really about the limiting beliefs they have. So, for coaches trying to build bigger businesses, they often think that they have to work ten times as hard and ten times the hours they're currently working to create a business that is ten times larger. They think that their niche is limited and there aren't enough potential clients. One of the *most* common limiting beliefs is that people won't be willing to spend the money for their coaching because it's too expensive for people. They believe that they don't have good enough marketing skills and that they can't learn digital marketing technology. They think they don't have enough resources—time, money, energy, team members—to build a big business. They don't know how to get started, and they don't have a specific plan or blueprint they can follow to create the coaching business they want. They may be starting with a very small list and think it will take forever to get a large one.

Ask yourself the same question about your Ideal Client. Write them all down. Next to each "obstacle" or limiting belief, write down specifically how you and your program can help them overcome it. Ask yourself, "How can I prove to them that I can help them with this problem?"

What do they *need* that they can't get anywhere else? Coaches and trainers can always find people to train them on their specific skill set. They can study with investors to learn about wealth creation. They can access all the research on parenting or communication skills. They can find courses on how to teach yoga or healthy eating. But once they have that skill set, they have no idea how to turn it into a viable business or how to scale up the business they already have to be even more successful and reach a larger audience. They have the skills to help thousands of people, but they don't have a system in place to reach those people. That's what they need, and that's what the Million Dollar Month Model offers them.

What do you (or could you) offer that your Ideal Client cannot get anywhere else? It needs to be something that is important to them and is critical to their success. If they don't know yet that it's critical to their success, you need to make sure that you make them understand how important it is. That is your Big Revelation. Napoleon Hill talks about the 16 success traits, and one of those traits is *specialized knowledge*. **The more you can show you have specialized knowledge, doing things other coaches/ trainers are not, the more you'll convert.**

What specific parts of my program will move the needle forward the most? Some of what I learned from my real estate coaching business is that we *all* need accountability. I also learned that people need constant mindset coaching, no matter how successful they have been. And I realized that people need help and lots of handholding in the beginning, to get themselves off to a good start. Once they make a good start and begin to get some wins under their belt, they don't need quite as much constant attention.

I offer the accountability piece (Skin in the Game, 37-day fast track program, etc.) in my real estate program. Another huge part of my real estate offer is the opportunity to co-author a book with me. They can use it in so many ways: They can use that book as an authority piece, as an education piece. They can use it before they go to a listing appointment, or they can use it to drop off after a listing appointment. If they are doing open houses, they can give it to prospective clients when they have an open house. I know that this one book can be used in so many different ways that will really move the needle for them in their business. And I know it's something they would never have thought about doing on their own—and that nobody else is offering. So, it's very unique and attractive to them.

Think about your own business. What will make the most impact and get them closer to what they want? During the event, you will need to seed these valuable pieces over and over again.

What will cost them a lot of time, energy, and money if they have to get to what they want on their own? I spent a ton of time, energy, and money figuring out the exact combination of pieces for the MDMM webinars and virtual events and the proper order these pieces need to be in. I learned it from paying for training from several of the top experts in sales, persuasion, and marketing. I also learned it from trial and error—and some of those errors were very costly! It would cost someone at least a million dollars to learn all that I now know, not to mention the money they'd *lose* while they were trying to figure it out! We also give them our CRM software that took thousands and thousands of dollars and countless hours for me and my team to develop. And it isn't just the money I've spent. It's all the resources, energy, time away from family, emotional and intellectual energy, etc., that they *won't* have to spend if they learn from me. They also won't have as much risk as I did. I had to put a lot on the line to do this, and I had to do it *without* the clear path I'm giving them.

In what you teach, if people try to figure out how to get what they want on their own, how much would it cost them? Where will they lose the most time, energy, and money? If you think about the time, energy, and money you spent yourself to get where you are, that will give you a sense of what it will cost them.

What will take them a lot of time or money to create? For coaches (the Ideal Client for my MDMM program), it would take them a ton of time to create slides for all the different parts of the presentation. If they don't have a fully robust CRM to handle everything they need (which most of them don't), it will take them months and thousands of dollars to have one created for them. Figuring out all the puzzle pieces and sequence to get the best result out of their trainings would take them literally years if they have to do it by trial and error. Getting a sales team up to speed would take them months, and in the meantime, they would lose potential clients who could have become clients with a well-trained sales team. Developing their funnels, email copy, swipe files, the SOPs (standard operating procedures) for every position and employee, the handbooks and brochures—all of this would take hundreds of hours and millions of dollars to create on their own. I know because we've spent millions to make millions!

What will cost your Ideal Client a ton of money and/or time to create on their own? Often, it's easy to see if your program is about business, but you can calculate it in other areas, too. For example, if they had to research menopause solutions or figure out what works by trial and error, how much time and money would it take? If they had to figure out how to make their marriage work, how much time and money would they spend in going to counseling or other trainings that doesn't get them the result you can get them? How much would a divorce cost them in attorney fees, and how much would they lose if they ended up divorcing and had to split up all their assets? How would it mess up their kids' lives?

What do they HATE doing that you can solve for them? For MDMM, I know that coaches are usually great with people, but they're usually *not* so great with systems and organization. They typically don't like dealing with details like figuring out the best equipment to use or how to schedule their trainings. They often resist sales and marketing. Most of them don't know how to overcome internal and external limiting beliefs, how to seed the offer, and seed the belief. I need to show them how to price marinate and how to be *in love* with making their offer rather than being hesitant about it. I need to help them love selling and help them know that *selling is service.*

Think about your Ideal Client and what they need. What do they absolutely hate doing that you could handle for them? Do they hate research? Do they hate numbers? Do they hate designing graphics or making presentations?

What do they have no idea about? The Ideal Client for my MDMM has no idea how to create or monetize their coaching/training business. They don't know where to start or what they need to get started. They don't know where or how to market. They definitely don't know how to properly structure the virtual trainings so that people convert and join their full program. They don't know how to make their business sustainable so that it keeps growing month after month. They don't know how to structure their business so that it can run smoothly and keep producing without them. They might be an influencer with a large list, but they are not monetizing it. I am shocked about how little influence influencers actually have. They are often not doing well financially. But if they had the right offer, they could be making millions, too.

What doesn't your Ideal Client know? Maybe they don't know how to bring in new clients or how to turn clients into raving fans. Maybe they don't know how to communicate with their spouse during conflicts. Maybe they've never learned how much their diet can affect their symptoms of menopause.

Get Input. Another way to approach this if you feel uncertain is to get feedback from your top 10 clients. Ask them: What have been the most impactful, powerful, and effective parts of your work with them? What are the top 5-8 things that your clients have learned from you and implemented that got them the most wins and helped them see the most results? What saved them the most time and money? What improved their lives the most? What will they never, ever forget from their work with you because it turned out to be so crucial to them?

Put the Pieces Together

Once you've done all the work to answer the questions above, take a look at the materials you've already created. Be honest and ask yourself, "Do these pieces really provide what they want and need? Are they truly unique and something that people can't get someplace else? Would they be irresistible to your Ideal Client?" You'll probably find that some of your material makes the cut and other pieces don't because those pieces don't make much difference to your Ideal Client, or they can get it anywhere. You don't have to throw out pieces that don't show up in your offer. You can still use them in your program if they offer real value. Just don't include them in your Irresistible Life Changing Offer. You want everything in your offer to be "Wow!" not just clutter.

Next, ask yourself what you're missing. What are you *not* offering that would make a tremendous difference to potential clients? What could you create, like a workshop or support system or blueprint, that would make a huge difference in helping them through obstacles? For example, we created implementation workshops because we saw that people weren't implementing. We added a 37-day fast track program for new students where they get extra hand-holding and coaching so they start off running. We added daily 15-minute accountability huddles, which help them fast-track their results like crazy and get them to implement more quickly.

Once you've seen what you're missing, start creating new resources that solve your clients' problems and help them get what they want. Make sure that you are customizing these resources so your Ideal Client recognizes that you really understand what they specifically want and need. Get creative and come up with powerful "how-to" solutions for them. For example, for the sales team training I include in my offer, I'd say, "How to get your own sales team up to speed quickly." Examples for other businesses could be: "How to communicate with your spouse during an argument." "How to get the testimonials you need to market your yoga studio." "How to connect with decision-makers in large corporations." "How to market yourself as a keynote speaker to large organizations."

The types of resources you'll create for your Ideal Client depend on what your program is about. Some of your resources will be DFY (done *for* you), and others will be DWY (done *with* you). In both of my coaching programs, it's all DWY. For example, for my MDMM program, we give them a funnel and teach them how to use it, but they put it together themselves and are responsible for changing the colors and copy, setting up all the sequences and triggers (DWY). When we give them our Value Creation Workshop, it's another DWY resource. You can create group solutions or one-on-one resources. My MDMM students get weekly *group* calls with different members of my team for coaching on topics like marketing, systems, sales, mindset, and video production. For an additional fee, they can also get one-on-one coaching where the head of my sales team trains their specific sales team, and they can get individual help with creating their offer, the Big Revelation, etc.

Other resources you could include would be things like checklists, PDFs, handbooks, books, podcasts and interviews, video scripts, access to an exclusive FB group, video or conversation scripts, self-paced video trainings, special seminars, accountability groups, weekly Zoom trainings, in-person summits. When you come up with these things, make sure that they are something you can provide on an ongoing basis. For example, in the contract for my real estate coaching, I tell them that for their weekly group coaching sessions, I will personally teach two times per month. I actually end up teaching twice a week, but I don't want to set that as the expectation. My calendar gets busy with speaking engagements and sessions for my new MDMM coaching business, not to mention family commitments. So, I want to make sure I can honor whatever we put in the contract. I always want to under-promise and over-deliver.

Make sure that anything you include in your Irresistible Life Changing Offer is something they are dying to get their hands on. Don't just throw in extras that aren't compelling to make it look like they're getting more. You'll just overwhelm them, and they'll start to think your program is too difficult or time-consuming for them. Be very strategic about what you put into your offer.

Bonuses are great to add in to get people to take action more quickly. Bonuses are on top of your core offer so that people feel like they're getting even more value by being decisive and enrolling during the event. The bonuses that you want to offer are things that they can't get anywhere else, and that they can't get outside of your offer—or if they can, it would be extremely expensive. Many times, the bonuses would really cost as much as the price of the offer itself. You can create your own bonuses or get high-value bonuses from others who are in compatible industries. Others benefit from giving away a part of their product or service to your clients because once they're exposed to the bonus, your people might eventually want to work with them more closely.

Based on what I know about my Ideal Client for my Million Dollar Month Model, this is the Irresistible Offer I put together:

- <u>2-Day Intensive Training with me</u> (to put all the pieces together for them, includes workbooks)

- <u>Value Creation Workshop</u> (where we work one-on-one with people to help them create their Irresistible Life Changing Offer and identify their Big Revelation)

- <u>Sales Funnels</u> (we've done over $57 million online—at the time I'm writing this book—and have 11 $1+ million dollar funnels)

- <u>Swipe Copy for Ads and Emails</u> (all of which have proven to convert)

- <u>Custom CRM</u> (developed specifically for coaches)

- <u>Sales Team Training</u> (where the head of my sales team works directly with their team to get the best results)

- <u>Marketing and Ads Team Training</u> (with our marketing team and our ad expert to show them the strategies we use to drive traffic)

- <u>Implementation Workshops</u> (for each piece of the MDMM program, including event training)

- <u>Daily Game Changer Accountability Sessions</u> (with myself or others on my team)

How to Showcase Your Irresistible Life Changing Offer

The key is to make sure that they understand each and every piece of what it is that you are offering before you make your offer. They need to *know why th*ey need it, how they are going to use it, and how it will help them and change their lives and/or their business. When you make the offer itself, you're not explaining what things are, how they can use it, and how it will help them. They absolutely already know. This is essential and key. You do this using all the techniques I talked about in Chapter 5. It's crucial that they know what it is that they are investing in and how it will change their life. Nothing in your offer should be guesswork to them. They know exactly what everything is.

Once you've identified the most important parts of your offer, you "reverse engineer" them into your trainings and everything you do. For example, if part of your Irresistible Offer is a self-paced 12-segment video training, you'll gather testimonials and case studies that highlight the results people got as they worked through the 12 segments. If your offer includes group accountability calls, you'll seed the importance of accountability through stories and examples. If you offer a custom CRM, you'll talk about the importance of having a great CRM and what it will cost them if they don't have one. You can also mention how much it cost you to put these different pieces together. During the segments of your trainings where you're giving them specific tips and tools, position each piece as a necessity for their success. You'll teach them enough about it so that they get value. But you won't give them all the ingredients and "how-tos" that are in your program. You'll just showcase the parts of your offer on a pedestal and give them a taste so they crave it.

When you put together a truly Irresistible Offer, you make it *impossible* for potential clients to compare you to your competition, and that makes you immune from price comparison. An Irresistible

Offer gives them (and you) the conviction that your services are worth every penny of their investment and more. They are so convinced that you are exactly what they need to get to their perfect ending that they'll find a way to pay for your services no matter what.

In the next chapter, I'll explain how and when to present your offer.

MDMM Mindset: Hard Now or Hard Later

Jerry Rice, who played with the NFL for 20 years, always said, "Today I will do what others won't, so tomorrow I can do what others can't." You and the people you plan to coach or train have to accept that it's not easy, especially in the beginning, to make the changes you want to see. It's hard, and it takes work. In the beginning, you usually don't see much in terms of results. You might feel out of your depth like you don't really know what you're doing.

But if you *don't* do what you need to do today, if you don't build the groundwork and foundation, where will you be one year from now, five years from now, or ten years from now? Will you still be exactly where you are with your business and in your personal life? Personally, I believe that if we aren't growing, we're actually heading backward, not just standing still. And I'm telling you (and you need to tell your clients) no one is coming to save you. It's up to you. So, do the hard work now. In my manifesto, it says, "You are the only one responsible for creating the life that you deserve. And you deserve it."

CHAPTER 7

Your Virtual Trainings

Million Dollar Month Model events are specifically designed to have people say "yes" to your program, in other words, to "convert" them. In this chapter, I'll tell you exactly how to put the pieces together to get there. One thing I won't talk about is your tactical or strategic content. My expertise has been real estate, and now I'm training coaches in the Million Dollar Month Model. I can tell you exactly what people need to learn to be successful in those two areas and what content will be useful and inspiring to them. But I *don't* have your expertise in running a successful dental practice, or how to be a great parent, or how to improve your golf game.

As I walk you through the webinar and 3-day virtual event, I want you to visualize yourself doing it. You might still have doubts that you really could do it. You may have even talked to friends or family who don't think you could or should do it. They may be well-meaning, but if expanding your reach as a coach or making a high ticket offer has been on your mind and in your heart, you need to pursue it despite your doubts and their bad advice.

I was 46 years old when I made the decision that I wanted to be a coach. I had been reading *Think and Grow Rich,* and the book talked about how we often have this constant nagging from the Universe telling us to do something. I knew for me it was coaching, but my career in real estate was going so well that I just kept pushing it back, ignoring the nudge.

But I was at a point in my life where I was ready. I just jumped on it. I had a meeting with my dad and mom (two of my most favorite people in the world) and my husband Steve (the love of my life and of course, another of my most favorite people in the world). I sat down to tell them about my plan to become a coach. And they said, "Krista, we love you. But you really should think about this. Normal people don't leave at 46 years old to change careers when they're bringing home over a million dollars a year. No one is going to pay you to coach them. It's just not a good idea. We love you; we know you're amazing, but you should really rethink this."

My dad, my mom, and my husband are the people who love me and support me the most, who want the best for me, and truly are my biggest fans. They were trying to help me and protect me. But literally, if I had listened to them and their advice and not gone with my true gut instinct, the Universe pulling me into the direction of coaching, I would not be where I am right now. And quite frankly, I would be miserable because I was at a point in my career where I was totally exhausted and tired. I didn't even realize just how exhausted and tired I was until I left the day-to-day of real estate and I was able to coach full-time.

Had I not listened to my gut and my heart and the Universe pulling me, had I listened to the people who really love me and wanted to help me, I would not be nearly as happy as I am now. I was happy before, but now I feel so fulfilled and like I'm making a real contribution. The more that I contribute to the world, the more I'm growing. Plus, rather than bringing in over $1 million *per year*, I was able to build a business that generates that much more *per month*. (I have 50 people working for me, so that's not all take-home pay. But it's still not shabby!)

I love my family, and they're all successful and brilliant in their own way. But none of them have ever built multi-million dollar businesses. In getting advice about building a coaching business, I needed to talk to people who were already successful doing it at the level I wanted. They had the best intentions, but my family was giving me bad advice.

One of my students for MDMM was great with AI (Artificial Intelligence). I asked him to do a training with my real estate students because I knew it would be useful and save them all a lot of money and time. He had *never* sold anything before, and he had a coach who told him, "Don't present at Krista's training. You are not ready to make an offer. It's too soon." I basically told him it was the worst advice *ever* and that he should fire his coach (which he did) and make his offer to my students. I coached him through it, and guess what? He closed at a 52% close ratio and made over $262,000 in this one training. The month prior, he couldn't even afford to pay his rent! If he had taken that bad advice from the coach who fed his fears and doubts, he would still be in the same position. You've got to start. His offer was a low-ticket offer, and it was his first time ever making an offer. And he still kicked some serious butt! He did it on Zoom with no fancy equipment. He just took massive effective action using a good offer and gave a great training. Do what he did, and Do It NOW!!!

Key Elements to Conversion

You'll be using the fundamental elements of conversion that I've mentioned throughout this book. One of the big mistakes I see most coaches make is that they'll hit one of these elements once or twice and think they're done. No! You need to present and seed them several times and in different forms (through stories, testimonials, statistics, etc.). Repetition is the key to mastery (and conversion) for them. And because repetition is the key to mastery for you as well, let's review these critical elements again:

Belief in themselves: I honestly don't know anyone who has rock-solid belief in themselves all the time in all areas! I've known amazing teachers who don't think they're smart enough to build a business.

I've known brilliant entrepreneurs who have no confidence in their parenting skills. These limiting beliefs sound like *I'm too old* or *I'm too young. I'm not attractive enough,* or *I'm not smart enough. I've never been good at XYZ,* or *I've failed at this before, so I'll probably fail again. I'm not good with technology,* or *People won't like me because of my accent,* or *I'm too new to this and don't have enough experience.* Your job is to figure out the common limiting beliefs of your Ideal Customer and then make sure you nail them during the events using the MDMM persuasion techniques and concepts (Chapter 5).

External limiting beliefs: This includes things like advice they get from friends, family, spouses, co-workers, people they hang out with, etc. Even though these advice-givers have usually not been successful themselves, their bad advice still has a lot of impact. Other external beliefs can be *I can't succeed in this economy,* or *The divorce statistics prove that it's nearly impossible to have a great marriage,* or *My competitors are all better/more experienced than I am,* or *I don't have the time/resources* or *I can't do it while my kids are young.* Even *The planets are in retrograde, so I shouldn't try anything new!* Again, you'll find specific beliefs that your Ideal Customers use to explain why they *can't* succeed. Address them and show how they are false. Often, you can show them others who succeeded despite those external obstacles.

You'll find that the top three external beliefs that almost everyone has are money, time, and spouse/business partner. *I don't have enough money to do it. I'm so swamped already that I can't imagine where I'd find the time. My spouse/business partner doesn't think it's a good idea.* People will use the excuses of time, money, or spouse/partner, but typically, it's really about fear, shame, and self-doubt, which leads to a lack of decisiveness. It's really important that you help them identify those real reasons in themselves. The virtual event itself is designed to get them over the fear and to believe in themselves even though they have shame and self-doubt. Make sure to deal with the real internal reasons (fear, shame/self-doubt, and lack of decisiveness), plus the external beliefs that are general to everyone (time, money, spouse/business partner), along with ones that are specific to what you're teaching.

Belief in the vehicle: This begins in your marketing through your ads, social media posts, emails, webinars, etc., and then continues throughout your virtual events. Every time you present some great content, you'll follow up with a testimonial about how that specific component helped one of your students. During the virtual events when you present a tip or strategy, you'll get participants to acknowledge that it could make a difference in their lives. (Remember the $75,000 idea from Chapter 5?) They need to be *certain* that your program will work for them—not just any program but *your* program. All they need to do is put in the effort and follow the system.

What you offer, your vehicle, is *exactly* what they need to get the result they are after. Showcase this over and over throughout your webinar and virtual event. They need to know exactly what your vehicle is, why they need it, how it will help them to get what they want, save or make them more money, save them time, improve their health, create positive relationships, be better parents, or whatever it is that you're teaching.

Belief in you: They have to believe in your sincerity and that you can help them. They need to understand that doing it on their own will be almost impossible, or at least very time-consuming and expensive. But when they do it with your guidance and support, if they do the work, they *will* get the result they want.

They also need to like you, trust you, know that you are authentic, and know that what you offer is something specific to you. They need to feel a connection to you. You can create this connection by bringing them into the conversation, relating what you're talking about back to them and their situation. You need to absolutely know who they are and speak in a manner where they feel as though you're speaking directly to them. When you hear them say, "I feel like you were speaking directly to me," you know you're connecting with them. They've got to feel like you get them, understand them, see them, and basically, you *are* them.

Seeding the offer: Another big problem I often see is that people don't seed the offer enough during the virtual events. It's as if they think they have to hide the offer and then spring it on event participants at the end. No! Potential clients need to know what you are offering. Seed your offer by showing them throughout the event all the different things that they need that are a part of your offer. For example, for my real estate coaching, I'll show them the marketing plan, co-author book, funnels, accountability program (Skin in the Game), seller's guide, buyer's guide, marketing video, and how to use Facebook ads.

One of the most important things I emphasize is how important being in the right rooms is, that it's the *who,* not just the *how.* I showcase that they'll get access to hundreds of agents across the country who are on the same path as they are and who are going after the same things. I talk about the importance of being with other people in a mastermind because that is a part of my offer. During my offer, I don't just spring it on them that they get access to a community. I've seeded and explained the importance of being in a mastermind and how it can help them. I'll bring up the book from Dan Sullivan and Ben Hard, *Who Not How,* and Napoleon Hill's *Think and Grow Rich,* both of which talk about how important a mastermind is and what it is. Throughout the event and before I make my offer, they have already seen how important a community is to their success.

I seed everything from the co-author book to the marketing plan to our community as a mastermind by teaching about these things throughout the training. By the time I make my offer for the program, they know exactly what each piece is, why they absolutely need it, and how it will change their life and business. I showcase these things over and over again, so when I finally make the Irresistible Life Changing Offer nothing is a surprise.

What I've seen people do is showcase a strategy or piece that is useful but then never go back to it again. You need to showcase pieces of your program over and over throughout the event so that there is no question about why they need those things. And remember, these are *not* just tangible things like books, pads, funnels, apps, and resources. It's also the community, office hours, support, accountability, in-person events, etc. Every aspect of your offer has to be seeded so they understand why it's so important. I emphasize this because, too often, I see presenters throw in some bonus when they make their offer that no one has ever heard of before. People have no idea why they would want or need that bonus.

People show up to your events because they know they need help, and they think that maybe you can help them. They know (or should know) that you've got a program to offer that will teach them much more than you could ever teach in a 90-minute Webinar or a 2-3 day virtual event. You want to show them that you have a specific system that will get them the results they're looking for. It's the reverse engineering we talked about in Chapter 6, taking parts of your offer and incorporating aspects of it into your trainings. You need to give them enough content so that they can experience for themselves how valuable your program would be for them. You'll be doing this consistently throughout the 2-3 day virtual event using the techniques and concepts in Chapter 5.

Repetition is not just important for the elements I mentioned above. Look back at Chapter 5, which talks about the MDMM puzzle pieces. All of the concepts we talked about there—like dealing with fear, investment versus liability, how the brain works and how to train it, the Big Revelation—are so important! Even though it seems like a lot to fit in, you *can't* skip anything. It will take some practice to really nail each piece. But once you figure out your rhythm and sharpen your presentation, you'll see how it all makes sense. *And* you'll see how following the Million Dollar Month Model gets you the amazing results you want. You won't be pulling teeth to get clients. People will be eager to say "yes" to you.

YOU Are the Main Event

It might feel intimidating, but during the 90 minutes of your webinar and during the 3-day virtual event, *you* are the star. Some people love getting in front of groups and having all of the attention focused on them. That was not me. Speaking in front of groups terrified me. Remember the story about when I was so nervous I said my own name wrong? But I knew if I wanted to do this business and fulfill my mission of helping people achieve success in their lives, I needed to step up to the plate.

I've spent literally hundreds of hours and thousands of dollars learning how to become a better, more effective speaker. But I was building a healthy business before I learned all of that. So, just keep in mind that you do *not* have to be perfect, and you will get better. But you do have to start. I see people wait so long to start because of fear. They don't want to make mistakes. They want to make it perfect.

The problem is you can't improve if you don't just start, and you'll learn so much as you go. So Do It Now!!!

Your main mission is to grab their attention and keep it! This is important whenever you're in front of an audience, but even more critical with a virtual audience! When you're presenting in person, they're trapped. They can still drift off, but at least they'll stay in the room, if only to be polite. When the presentation is virtual, and they're at home or in their office, they have tons of potential distractions. Even if you tell them to be somewhere that they won't get interrupted and to turn off their cell phones, it's still easy for them to wander off. It's like the difference between watching a movie at the theater or watching it at home. At the movie theater, if a movie is just okay, you'll probably stick it out until the end. If you watched the same movie at home, you'd probably get up and put a load of laundry in, or check on the latest sports scores, or even just turn it off.

Grabbing and keeping their attention virtually takes more energy. It starts with you and your passion for what you're teaching. If you show them that you are really enthusiastic about what you're teaching and sincere about helping them, they'll feel it and want to listen to you. If you prove to them that you can teach them something that will significantly improve their lives, they'll be eager to give you their precious attention to learn from you.

When you're virtual, it's like you have to reach into the camera and grab them through their screens. Most presenters need to be more animated than they're used to. Personally, I always stand when doing my webinars and virtual events. Even before I had a studio and just did these presentations on Zoom, I'd arrange the camera so that I could stand and move around a little bit. It gives me more freedom to gesture, and it keeps my energy up. I'm able to show confidence in my posture and excitement in my eyes more. (BTW, your posture says so much about how you're feeling! Make sure it's saying what you want it to say!) I tend to be pretty animated anyway, but when I'm standing and moving, I notice that I'm more expressive in my whole body, including my face. A speaker who stands and moves and gestures is much more interesting to watch than a talking head seated in front of a camera looking down at their notes.

And research shows that when people can see your hands, they trust you more. So, make sure your hands can be seen during your events. For example, when you mention the name of someone who is powerful and successful and then touch your heart or yourself (not in an inappropriate way!), your audience will associate that successful person with you because you're saying their name while pointing at yourself.

Test it for yourself. Try recording yourself seated, then record yourself standing with some room to move as you talk. Notice the difference in your eyes and face. How are you holding your body differently? Is there a difference in your tone and volume? Being seated might feel safer and more comfortable, but I doubt that you're as animated, energetic, enthusiastic, and expressive as when you're up and moving.

I'm not telling you to be what you aren't, just to amp up who you are so that it comes across on their screens. We all have a personal style, and you want yours to shine through more. Personally, I'm fast-paced, funny, casual at times, dynamic, passionate about what I teach, and determined to help them learn it. I smile a lot. I talk fast. I like to wear fun clothes and cute shoes. I'm very expressive with my voice, sometimes to the point where I lose my voice after the 3-day virtual event. This is my style, and it works for me. It wouldn't work at all if I tried to be someone else. You need to be you and honor your style as well. The idea is to express even more of who you are.

Another big key to grabbing and keeping their attention is the clarity and impact of what you're presenting. In the virtual world, it's especially important to make your main points clear and memorable. In person, you may be able to wander off on a tangent, but too many tangents during a virtual event will just lose and confuse them. Keep in mind that people learn differently. Some are visual learners; some are auditory. Some people learn by facts and figures, some through stories. You can't just make an important point once and call it done. You have to repeat it and tackle it from different angles to really get the point across and make it memorable.

One technique that helps with clarity is to number your main points. For example, "5 Keys to Communicating with Your Spouse" or "4 Building Blocks to a Successful Dental Practice." I use this for every piece I teach. It not only helps them organize what I'm teaching in their brains, but it also keeps me on track as I'm teaching. Another technique is just to tell them that this point is important to them. I'll say, "Write this down," or "You're going to want to remember this," or "If you only learn one thing today, this is it."

Another cool thing to do is to create frameworks for concepts or tactics. For example, I teach a time/focus management practice that is based on the Pomodoro Technique but a little different. I call mine Success Sprints. I teach them to do 30-minute time blocks throughout the day on whatever they're working on. Then I have them take a three-minute break and then do a few minutes to THRIVE. "T" stands for give *thanks* and show gratitude. "H" is for *happy,* so I have them laugh out loud. "R" is *reminding* themselves that they have all the resources that they need. "I" means to take *immediate* action, "Do it NOW!" "V" is to *visualize* the results they want as already accomplished. And "E" is to *expect* it, be *enthusiastic* about it, and have *energy* around it. THRIVE is a framework that makes it "sticky" and easy to remember.

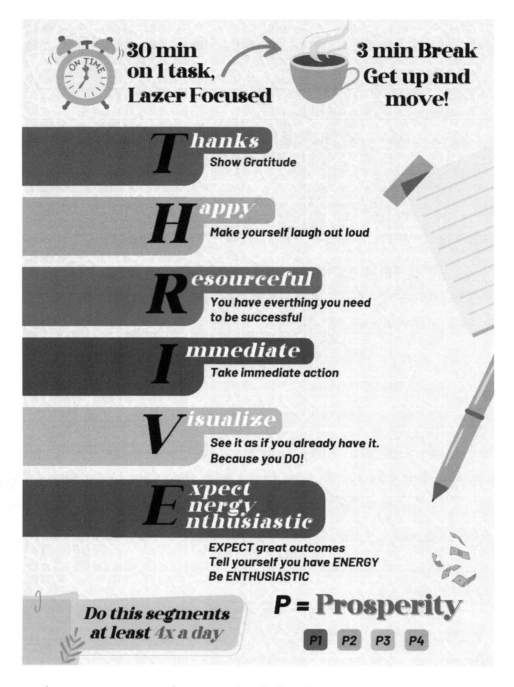

Stories are also a great way to make a point "sticky" and memorable. They can be real-life stories or fiction as long as they *clearly* make the point you're teaching. When you tell a story, it works best if you put some drama into it. Paint a picture for them. Have a plot where a lot is at risk for the hero or heroine. Use gestures and emotional words when telling the story. Help them relate to the story with questions like, "Can you imagine how that felt?" "Have you ever been in that situation?"

I also use a lot of graphics in PowerPoint to get points across as I'm speaking. I've learned to do a balance of just me on the screen, just the graphic on the screen, and me and the graphic on a split screen. You'll lose them if you just show them slide after slide of boring text on full screen. They need to see you, and they need to see things that are visually interesting to keep their attention.

To keep their attention, you also need to bring them into the conversation and keep them active using some of the techniques we talked about in Chapter 5. Ask them questions and get them to put their answers in the chat. Have them pull out their workbooks and do an exercise. Have them raise their hands when they agree with something. One great way to get them and keep them engaged (I mentioned it in Chapter 5) is to create a group identity that they can relate to. For example, to my real estate audience, I'll say, "There are Doers and Dabblers in this world. Dabblers never fully commit. They just play at this business. Doers are serious about the business and want to do what it takes. And I can tell that all of you are Doers because you showed up to learn something." Then, throughout the event, I'll remind them: "We're Doers, right?" The group identity helps keep them engaged and also makes them feel good that they are part of a special group and you've recognized them for it.

Again, the order of each piece makes a huge difference. After tracking dozens of trainings, tweaking and rearranging pieces, we have a formula that really works. I'm giving you the overview of both the webinar and 2-3 day virtual event here.

Webinar

For the first four years of my real estate coaching, I taught live 5-day trainings every month that lasted 60 to 90 minutes each day rather than one 90-minute webinar. It was exhausting! I put a lot of time and energy into every single one, and though they were effective, I felt like I couldn't maintain that pace and keep presenting fresh material. I also started having trouble with my voice, even losing it completely at one point! We decided to test out a 90-minute webinar called "What's Working Now in Real Estate." And you know what? Our conversion rate to the 3-day virtual event was almost *exactly the same.* We also found that people who didn't convert during their first webinar with us would come back in the following months to see what new trends we were going to talk about. Eventually, many of those ended up converting. So, what I recommend to my MDMM students now is to do the webinar, and they're experiencing the same success. In fact, I recommend that they do a few webinars in between each 3-day event to get more registrations and to build up their lists.

One thing we discovered is that, as long as they went to the 3-day event, it didn't matter if they went to the webinar or not. Conversions into the program from the 3-day event were the same whether they went to the webinar or not. We tested this for several months, and it didn't make a difference. But we do the webinar because the cost per lead (CPL) was less expensive getting people to register for the webinar. It allowed us to get their email addresses to add to our list.

The show up rate to a free webinar is much lower. That is why it is still important to drive traffic *directly* to the 3-day event because, since they are paying, show up rate is significantly higher. I do a webinar instead of a 5-day challenge now because not only did it take way less time and energy out of me, but also conversions and CPL were better.

You'll see that the webinar's content is built around 3 Secrets that I learned from Jason Fladlien and Russell Brunson (or, as I like to call them, 3 Forces). Why? You've only got 90 minutes, and you want to make sure that they have some actionable learning during that time. If you try to teach more than three main points, you won't be able to go into enough depth on any of them. So, keep it simple. Figure out three of the best strategies in your program and use those as your secrets. For each secret, first give the overview. Next, give them specific examples or tactics. Finally, show them success stories or testimonials for each tactic.

Each of the "3 secrets" is not only a tactic they can use, but it's also designed to address their excuses or obstacles and support your Big Revelation. The "3 secrets" are about the three things that you are trying to get them to believe. You're trying to get them to believe in the Big Revelation and knock down every reason or obstacle that is preventing them from believing in it.

With *Secret #1*, you teach a tactic or strategy that supports the specific vehicle (your program) that you want them to believe in, as well as giving them belief in you as the person they need to help them.

Secret #2 will be a tactic or strategy that relates to their limiting beliefs about external obstacles to getting what they want.

Secret #3 will be a training that helps them begin to believe in themselves by addressing internal limiting beliefs. The reason the framework works so well is that each of the secrets works to knock down whatever is keeping them from taking action.

For example, in my real estate coaching, I want to get them to believe and understand the Big Revelation that if they want to be a top-producing agent, they need to become a top marketer. I have to get them to identify as a totally different person, not an agent selling houses but a master marketer. The vehicle to becoming a top producer and master marketer is using video and paid ads to get traffic. So, for Secret #1 (the vehicle) I teach them how to create videos that convert through paid ads on social media. For Secret #2 (internal belief), I teach them how to break through fear and resistance and finally feel confident in front of the camera, even if they are shy and introverted. For Secret #3 (external belief), I teach them how to create a professional video in under 10 minutes using free apps (addressing their external beliefs about not enough time or money).

I always try to do these webinars live and I don't use my emcee for them. I do them live because it's been proven time after time that live webinars convert more. You're able to make connection, call out people's names, see their faces, dive deeper when they look lost, or expand more when they are nodding their heads. That said, there is software out there that makes it look and appear more live without being dishonest about it. This is great because it would allow you to do webinars more often and increase the number of people going to the 3-day event. My team and I are currently testing these resources out. (I'll let you know my results and possibly add them to the resource page Theprovenmodel.com/resources after we've tested and have more concrete info and statistics on that.)

Scan this QR code using the camera app on your phone to access your resource page & added freebies now!

You don't need an emcee because it's live, and you're the one running it. Since I'm introducing myself, I keep it brief, but I still highlight all the things that make me stand out (the books I've written, my awards in real estate and in digital marketing, impressive stats about my accomplishments, the media where I've been featured, and photos of me with influential people like Tony Robbins, Russell Brunson, Alex Hormozi, Elena Cardone, Brad Lea, and Dean Graziosi). I also make sure they know that I've achieved what they want to achieve, and I've helped others get what they want as well. I do this because it gives me more authority and status. When people see that, they think, *Oh, she must know what she's talking about if she's hanging out with those heavy hitters.* The accomplishments and awards automatically elevate my status as an expert digital marketer. It gives people a reason to want to keep listening to me. We do this on both webinar and 3-day, and it's very effective.

I've done these webinars at different times of day and on different days of the week. I try to avoid times and days when my Ideal Client is usually busy (for real estate agents, this is often weekends and evenings). Try different times/days and track your attendance to see if some time slots are better than others.

I like to start out strong with a Bold Promise of the results they can get if they pay attention and implement what I'm about to teach them. For example, I might say, "I promise you that at the end of these 90 minutes, you'll have three new strategies that can double the number of listings you get next month if you implement them." Because the webinar is free, people usually show up with the attitude, "Let's check in for a few minutes to see if this is worth my time." So, you need to grab their attention immediately by letting them know that they'll be learning something that will really help them get to their dream outcome.

3-Day Bootcamp

The reason we went from 2 days to 3 days is to give logical buyers more time to intellectually justify the investment. Many people (like me!) are emotional buyers. We make decisions with our guts, our intuition. We don't need to know every tiny detail of what it is and how exactly it works. We just know we want it. But not everyone is like that. It's like buying a car. Some people will show up on the lot, drive a few vehicles, find the one they like, and drive it home that night. Other people will drive a vehicle, go home, look for reviews on the internet, talk to their neighbors, etc., before making a decision.

When I learned more about different types of decision-makers, we decided to test it and add an extra day so that analytical decision-makers had time to do their due diligence. You know what? Our conversions went up about 5.3%. We end up getting a LOT more booked calls to learn about our events between days 2 and 3 that would not have happened if we had not changed that. So now I highly recommend doing three days rather than just two. Now I know what you are thinking because I hear it all of the time: "My Ideal Client will not spend three days on a virtual event." But I find that to be wrong the majority of the time as long as the content is good and they are engaged and finding value in what you are providing. That's the key. Now, if you're dealing with super busy multi-millionaires who have literally no time, you may be right. In that case, try two days. We've had many months using 2-day events where we did over $1 million each time. But in most cases, you will convert more in 3 days because you'll convert more of the analytical buyers. Remember, MDMM is a system that we've been testing and tweaking to get the best results. Follow the system!

Right now, I do my virtual events on Monday, Tuesday, and Wednesday. But honestly, I like starting on Tuesday better. Why? Because that schedule works for people in real estate. On Fridays, they are typically gearing up for the activity they'll have over the weekend when their clients are most available. On Mondays, they are typically dealing with all the business that happened during the weekend. Many people run their virtual events on Thursday through Saturday. It all depends on your Ideal Clients and when they would be most available.

The reason we start on Mondays is that it sets me up to make the offer on Tuesdays. By doing this, my sales team can get through most of the calls that are booked by Friday evening. We've found that fewer calls are booked during the weekend, and there are more no-shows to the calls that are booked because Realtors® work during the weekend.

I have an emcee for this event. The main purpose of an emcee is to handle housekeeping, engage the audience, and give me a few breaks. Plus, if the event is a recording of a prior event (which is what I use for a few months once I've perfected it), the emcee makes it seem more live. Imagine having Million Dollar Months without even having to be present and allowing your team to work the event. It's super sexy. ;o)

The emcee brings the audience in to share "Ahas" and wins, which also helps with engagement and stay rate. The emcee also introduces me and shows all of my credentials, the books I've written, and my awards to tee me up. Finally, she shows an introduction video that we've created of me. It showcases my expertise on stages, speaking, and running my events. It helps gain trust and gives me authority, a "why you should listen to me" type video.

As I started to lay out all the pieces of the 3-day training, I realized that—yikes!—there is so much that goes into it! We run from 8:30 AM to 2:30 PM with a couple of short breaks and a 30-minute lunch, and I try to make every minute count. Most of the pieces of the virtual event serve a couple of purposes. I may teach a tactic that also seeds a part of my offer. Or I may tell a story about my life that helps them relate to me but also teaches a strategy.

Much of the morning of Day 1 is dealing with mindset. But you must still give them some strategy and tactics, or else the type A learners/high D personalities are going to get impatient and leave. It's a whole mix of doing just the right balance. We've learned after doing this so many times. I've changed my presentation so that I do some tactic or strategy that is really, really meaty within the first 60 minutes. Something that's going to make them want to come back and makes them realize, *Man, this is definitely worth my time.*

On Day 2, you want some really high-value strategy and tactic training in the morning. In fact, all of Day 2 is a lot more tactic and strategy than Day 1 because I really want to teach them things that will make a difference for them. Presenting lots of tactics and strategies also shows them the many gaps they have in their business and gives them high value (which I do throughout the event). In fact, one of my mentors told me, "Krista, in a webinar or 3-day event, it is impossible to really TEACH people how to do what you've spent years and thousands of hours to learn. Your job is to get them to believe in your program or vehicle, in themselves, and that they need you to help them."

That said, giving tactical strategies and "how-tos" is important, as is working with their mindsets throughout. It is imperative that you get this sequenced balancing act right, or you'll never be able to accomplish what we have. That is why my MDMM works so well. We've been obsessed with figuring it all out, and we have the results to prove time after time that it works. I'm making my offer on Day 2, so through teaching the tactics and strategies, I am letting them know all the things they're getting and have it be fresh in their mind. The mindset sections on this day are really focused on getting people to want to take action.

During Day 3, I talk a lot about decisiveness, one of Napoleon Hill's Success Principles. I want them to realize that the success of their business is determined by how decisive they are in taking action. And I want the people who still haven't booked a call to realize that it's a decision that could literally change their lives. We also do a deep dive that focuses on the 6 reasons why people don't buy:

1. Lack of Decision Making
2. Time
3. Money
4. Spouse/Partner
5. Fear
6. Shame and Self Doubt

It's important to touch on all of these and do activities around them to help people overcome these obstacles. Obviously, we do this all throughout the three days, but there is a high emphasis on this for Day 3.

Presenting Your Irresistible Offer

I present the offer before lunch on Day 2. For my real estate coaching business, right before my offer, I go over all the things I've been teaching them that are part of my program, and I compare it to what other agents know and do. "Here's you, and here's your competitor. Now imagine all these things, and you can see what a competitive edge this gives you. Can you see how this will work for you? Can you see how, if you have all these extra tools in your toolbox that you're able to utilize, you're going to be able to do more business?"

KRISTA	VS	OTHER AGENTS
20% Niche videos & ads		0%
50% Solution videos retargeting ads		0%
65% Nurturing videos retargeting ads		0%
75% What's My Home Worth CMA retargeting ads		0%
100% What's My Home Worth CMA Funnel		0%
150% Seller Seminar Funnel		0%
175% Drop off CMA Box		0%
275% Seller Reads My Marketing Plan		0%
325% Seller Reads My Seller's Guide		0%
500% Seller Reads My Savvy Seller Book		0%
600% Digital Follow Up Zoom CMA Review		0%
700% 17 Minute Video Listing Presentation		0%
800% Digital Delivery CMA Box PDFs		0%
900% Does It Matter Who Sells Your Home Video		0%
1000% Seller Testimoniala Previous Property Marketing Videos		0%

Remember, throughout the event, you've been relating whatever you present back to them, always having them rate themselves on their scorecards and having them do micro-commitments throughout the event.

I also remind them that at some point, they'll be competing with an agent who is using my system, and it is going to be impossible to beat them. I do this because #1, it's true, and #2, by nature, agents are very competitive (like we all are) and want to win. So, I'm seeding the fact of FOMO (fear of missing out) or FOLO (fear of losing out). They cannot compete against my agents and my system. Without it, they are going to fail, but with my system, they will succeed.

Next, I'll say, "Okay, look at the back of your workbook. How many $75,000 A-ha's and ideas do you have? Add it up and put it in the chat." They start putting in $800,000, $500,000, even $1.6 million. I'm getting them to see how much value they've gotten out of what I've taught them already. That way, when I make my offer, they're reminded of all the things they have already learned, and they're associating a monetary value to it. By the time I actually make my offer, I can say, "Hey, the cost is under

$24,000. You just got done telling me that you've already gotten ideas that can generate an additional $1.6 million or $800,000. Can you see by investing this $23,997 just how much it can move the needle in your business?" Next, I ask them again, "If you do nothing different, how will anything change?" I ask them to pull out their scorecards and notice all the things they are missing. Again, they are showing themselves what their weaknesses are without me pointing it out to them. And obviously, the scorecard lists everything they could get in my program.

As I ask these questions, I'm getting them to nod their heads and say yes out loud as often as possible. "Can you see how this can work? Can you see how your business would change by implementing all those $75k ideas?" These are micro commitments that get them in the habit of saying "yes," so they'll be more likely to continue to say "yes" to my Irresistible Life Changing Offer.

I then give them two options: Option 1: Do it all yourself. Option 2: Let us get you there. I show them exactly everything they're getting in the program and then add up its value (which is $190,989). Then I tell them that the cost today is $23,997. Because my program is about real estate, I can say, "How many homes would you have to sell?" and I do the calculations for them at different commission levels. I also compare it to a college education and the average earnings of a college graduate versus the money a really good agent can make.

After I've shown them the cost, I show them the bonuses and talk about their value. I learned this from Jason Fladlien. He points out that if you show them all the bonuses *before* you tell them the cost, they end up fixated on the cost. But if you show them the bonuses *after* the cost, they're thinking, *Wow. It was a good deal before, but if I act now, I get all these bonuses too!* They're focused on what they're *getting*, not what they're *paying*.

Next, I simply tell them to book a call (which we talked about in Chapter 2) as my Call to Action. At that point, I answer all the questions that (from experience and looking at the chat) I already know they will have.

Go back and review Chapter 2, where I talk about all the things you need to be tracking and optimizing to make sure that you get the results you want: The 7 Levers for 7 Figures.

MDMM Mindset: THRIVE

I talked about this above as something I teach my students. Now it's your turn because building an MDMM business takes focus! Set up your day in 30-minute time blocks with a specific area to work on in each block. Then, take a three-minute break. During that break, spend a few minutes to

THRIVE. "T" stands for give *thanks* and show gratitude. "H" is for *happy*, so go ahead and laugh out loud! "R" is to *remind* yourself that you have all the resources you need. "I" is *immediate* action, "Do it NOW!" "V" is to *visualize* the results you want as already accomplished. And "E" to *expect* it, be *enthusiastic* about it, and have *energy* around it. Do this system for two weeks, and you'll be amazed at how much you get done! (For a more complete training on THRIVE, go to Theprovenmodel.com/resources.)

Scan this QR code using the camera app on your phone to access your resource page & added freebies now!

Generosity Breeds Success

It's a Universal Law: The more you give, the more you get.

The more you encourage others to succeed, the more you will succeed.

The more value you offer, asking nothing in return, the more wealth will come to you.

And you know what's one of the easiest ways to do this right this moment? Give *My Guide to Million Dollar Months* a 5-star review so that others who want to make a positive impact in the world are encouraged to learn what you're learning.

Be generous. When one of us succeeds, we all succeed.

Thank you!

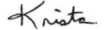

CHAPTER 8

Your MDMM Marketing Campaign

In this chapter, we're going to get into some of the nuts and bolts of digital marketing and how you can build your authority within your community. If you're already savvy about marketing online and you've already established yourself as an authority, great! But I'd suggest you read this chapter anyway because it's easy to become complacent and forget some of the basics. If you are new to this type of marketing and you're not yet established as an authority, great! I won't be able to teach you everything you need to know but this will give you a good starting point. Just keep in mind that you can get started with what you have and build up your authority as you go along.

If you really dove into Chapter 3—your Ideal Client, studying your competitors, and discovering your Big Revelation—you've got plenty of ammunition to start your marketing campaign. You know your Ideal Client's pain points and their dreams. You know where they hang out and what gets their attention. You've gotten tips from your competitors about messaging and what attracts potential clients. You've got your Big Revelation and can use it in everything you do.

Using the Power of Online Marketing

I teach entire programs about how to use social media and digital marketing for businesses. There's no way I'd be able to cover absolutely everything you need to know about it here! But (bottom line), to build your Million Dollar Month business, you need to be marketing online on social media platforms. That's just where the action is. That's where your customers are hanging out, and that's often where they make their buying decisions. And in terms of the bang you get for your buck (if you do it correctly), digital marketing is amazing.

If you are just starting in this type of marketing, don't get overwhelmed by it. Take it step by step. I suggest starting with just one platform at a time, like Facebook. Learn all you can about it. You'll find a ton of tutorials online. Then start with an ad, a video sales letter (VSL), a brief webinar, or a written blog and track your results (which may not be instant, so give it a little time). When you've done that, try something new, like a video blog or a Facebook Live. The key is consistency. Posting a blog once every two months will not get you any traction. You want to be a consistent presence on whatever platform you're using. Once you master and implement a platform, keep doing the one you've mastered as you add others. One of my taglines is "Learn, Implement, Master, Repeat." Keep in mind that technologies are changing constantly, so you'll need to pay attention to know when something new and improved shows up that can better reach your potential clients.

Just marketing on social media channels without paying for ads will not work in most cases. Less than .001% of posts go viral. There's a lot of noise on social media because it's so easy to post, and anyone can do it. It's become harder and harder than it used to be for a post to get attention. In my experience, the fastest way to get the attention you want is to pay for it. Think of attention as currency. The more attention you can get, the more money you'll make. So, you're going to have to invest your marketing dollars into getting more attention. The downside to paid ads is that you're held hostage to these sites and have to keep paying them (Facebook, etc.). More and more people are realizing the power of advertising on these sites because that's where their audience spends its time. So, the price of paid ads on social media keeps increasing. But without my ads on Facebook, I wouldn't have a business! When you market yourself organically using YouTube or blogs, it most likely will take longer, but the info is there forever, and you don't have to pay to keep it there.

Honestly, I love YouTube and am finally trying to dive more into that market. However, I will tell you that a little over five years into my business and hitting the $51 Million mark has been almost entirely through Facebook advertising. So, I'm a huge fan. However, I also know lots of marketers who swear by YouTube or TikTok. Pick your poison. Learn, Implement, Master, Repeat. After 5+ years of following that rule, I'm finally delving into other areas besides Facebook. So, I'm practicing what I preach!

If working with the technical side of digital marketing is just not your thing, hire someone to do it for you! Focus on creating great content instead and let someone else place what you create. You still want to stay on top of tracking the results they're getting for you, but you should be able to find someone good who can actually place ads and post videos and articles for you.

The beauty of digital marketing is that for each video and blog you create, you are creating a target audience. You're creating an *audience*, not targeting one person. You're showing up where people who might be interested in what you offer show up. Then, you'll redirect them to the next thing you want your audience to see. Anyone who ever looks at your videos, or reads your blogs, or who does any research on you becomes a part of your target audience. You'll start showing up in their feed, on their computer—anywhere they go, you'll be there.

Your Secret MDMM Weapon: Video

Video is hands down the most effective way to market. Even if you are a little bit shy, for a coach, I'd say it's mandatory. Something I always say is, ***"Be seen, be heard, be known."*** This is especially true in the coaching business. People need to know you before they sign up with you. Yes, you may have a specific program that you teach, but your real product is *you*. Your experience, your talent, and your knowledge are your product. Product videos help people make purchasing decisions for products, and since *you're* the product, they need to see videos of *you* giving them great content.

If you aren't totally sold on video yet, take a look at these 2023 stats:[2]

- In the US alone, 244.4 million people watch digital videos.

- 9 out of 10 consumers between 12 and 44 years old watch digital videos, and 97.8% of those who are 18-24.

- People over 65 are less likely to watch videos online but still 63.8% of them do.

- A 2023 study showed that 91% of consumers want to see more online video content from brands. (In 2018, 85% wanted more, so consumer attraction to videos is growing.)

- Recent video marketing stats show that 86% of marketing professionals use video as a marketing tool, and 78% say videos are directly responsible for increasing sales. 86% say that videos helped drive traffic to their website.

- A 2022 survey found that short-form videos are preferred by 66% of consumers over long-form videos. ("Short-form" and "long-form" are different depending on the platform. For example, Instagram feed videos are best at about 26 seconds, while Facebook videos that are 2-5 minutes get higher engagement.)

- In 2023, 92% of marketers said that videos gave a great return on investment (compared to 78% in 2018). 88% of marketers say that video has a better ROI than other marketing strategies.

- Video statistics show that viewers retain about 95% of the information from the video compared to 10% from reading the text.

- In their searches, Google users are most likely to click on a video search result.

- Nearly 93% of video marketers say they got new customers from videos posted on social media, and 83% generated leads using video.

- 33% of marketers say that their video marketing strategy is more important than their website.

---

[2] https://www.oberlo.com/blog/video-marketing-statistics

The statistics on the impact of using video in marketing are incredible! Video is the number one best thing that you can do to jumpstart your coaching business or expand your current coaching business or high ticket offer, even if you already have a good following. Why? ***Because your job is to get more people to know you, like you, and trust you. Your job is to break down the barriers, that lack of trust or belief we all have.*** The more you use video, the more that you become a real person to them. They start to feel they know you because they see you so often in your videos. This is called a parasocial relationship, and it is really the fastest way to get your potential clients to know and trust you. Think about your favorite TV show. You've got a character that you love. You cry for them, you cheer for them. You hate any bad guys that are against them. That's because you've developed a parasocial relationship with them. It's a one-sided relationship. You've never met them, and they don't know you, but you feel like you know them personally. That's the power of video.

My students often start out thinking that it takes too much time to create videos. But once you start doing it and get familiar with the process, it takes hardly any time at all. I can create a video now in less time than it takes to write an email or make a phone call! Just the other day, I created 16 videos (8 TikTok videos and 8 Facebook Videos for ads) in under 47 minutes. All you need is a good topic, any content that will make the life of your Ideal Client better somehow. Just come up with a problem they have (that they may not know about) and give them some tips on solving it. Or give them some good information that is relevant to their lives. This is another reason to deep dive into your Ideal Client.

Once you get going using the MDMM, you'll want a lot of different videos. You might find it easiest to set a day aside each week to record eight content videos for the month or four videos for the next two weeks. Ultimately, you'll want to get video content out daily, but this is a good start. Schedule a specific time slot when you won't get interrupted. Get the room set up and be all ready to go with ideas of what you're going to say. Then, for each video, you can change your clothes and even change your hairstyle. Recording multiple videos at one time is much less overwhelming for most people.

I encourage you to learn about AI by using ChatGPT or Jasper. AI can create a content calendar and give you scripts, etc., that are in your voice. It can save you a ton of time. Books upon books could be written about how much AI can help you in your business. I'll leave it to you to study for yourself. Just know that AI is there to help you, not hurt you. If you harness its ability instead of fearing it, you'll be amazed at how much AI can assist you.

With videos, shorter is better, but it depends on the platform and this changes. For example, on YouTube, they like longer videos. People tend to think they're getting a longer video when they go to YouTube. But YouTube shorts (short videos) are okay and work really well (for now, at least). In general, keep your videos under 30 seconds if you can and give as much value as possible within that time frame. Don't start by saying your name or introducing yourself. Start it with something really catchy. You have only 6 seconds to capture their attention—I am NOT kidding!—so don't waste seconds by saying your

MY GUIDE TO MILLION DOLLAR MONTHS

name. Hook them in immediately. For example, a Modern Mom coach might say, "I've got three huge tips that are going to save you so much time today." A coach for professional photographers might say, "I just learned this amazing trick that just landed me five new clients." Someone with a high ticket offer that is AI for Realtors® might say, "How would you like to generate a full market study for a potential listing in under 5 seconds?" After the catchy opening, then you can say your name and business name.

A few years ago, people said that a three-minute video was good. All the research now shows that 30 seconds or less is better. Studies show that 20% of people will leave after the first 10 seconds of watching a video. Yikes! So, you need to make sure that you're engaging and motivating them to continue watching.

If you are brand new to creating videos, find someone who has a similar program, who is well known, and who is attracting followers. This should be a big part of the research on your competition you did in Chapter 3. Watch videos and webinars of competitors who are successful. Read their content. *Emulate* what they're doing. Remember, this doesn't mean to plagiarize or to copy their material. That would be unethical, and you still want your own personality to shine through, and you want your own approach and spin on the topic. But you can follow somebody else who is using video well and notice what's working for them. If it's working for them, it can work for you. Make your competitors who are succeeding become your personal mentors. Learn from them, then create your own material.

A lot of people are afraid of being in front of the camera. They worry about having the right equipment and perfect setup (or the perfect nose). You just need to do it and get over any fear or hesitation you have about it. Today, I've got a videographer and his fancy cameras and a whole studio that I've built in my house. Did I start that way? Heck, no! I started making videos on my phone in my kitchen. Even now that I have a full-time videographer, the majority of my videos are just recorded with my phone without any editing at all. If I want to spruce up a video of my own, I use great plug-ins or apps that can add a few things very easily and quickly. Just do it and create a video every day. Send them to a friend or your mom and ask for feedback. If you don't just start, you never will.

Don't worry about the lighting or getting a tripod or the perfect backdrop. All of those are just excuses, right? Use your cell phone. Record yourself on Zoom. Push record and make sure you've got decent light (no crazy glare), good sound (no dogs barking in the background), and a suitable background (no undies hanging to dry behind you—though I guess it depends on your niche!) Then go for it. Your goal with these first videos is to just get comfortable. No one has to see them except the people you choose. Watch your own videos, and you'll see where you can improve. But don't be overly critical!

When I started being a coach, I was studying everyone and anyone to learn things. I was learning how to use webinar software, and one of my favorite online teachers was a guy who had a goofy haircut, often used the wrong words, and even picked his nose! But he was great! I learned a lot from him and could tell he was just being himself. And because of that, I trusted him and liked him. Research shows that the more someone sees you or watches your content, the more they learn to like you. You start to grow on people. So, you want to create as much content as you possibly can and add as much value as possible. The goofy guy I liked had the "3 Es": His videos were entertaining, educational, and engaging. That's all he needed, and that's all you need too! I now teach the "6 Es of video": Educate, Entertain, Excite, Enthusiastic, Engage, Encourage to Take Action. You can't always do them all, but the more you try to do them, the more you'll get engagement from people who want to take action and watch longer.

After you've done a few videos for practice to get comfortable, you're ready to start recording "for real." You can do a couple of takes, but do NOT try to be perfect! Just like that goofy guy, imperfect is much more engaging and relatable. It's okay to be perfectly imperfect. Just start and do it!

Problem to Solution: The Marketing Journey

One aspect of great marketing psychology is to identify a problem that your target market *doesn't even know they have*, point out to them *why* it is a problem, and *offer a solution* (your program). So, for example, let's just say your program is about helping solopreneurs create great websites and landing pages. One thing you might know that they don't know is that if they design their website with certain types of software, it loads more slowly. So, what's the problem with slower-loading software? How about if you were able to say, "Did you know that if your website takes 7 seconds to load or even longer than 3 seconds to load, you are losing 73% of customers that visit your website because people are too impatient to wait? People are bouncing off your website before they even see it because the loading time takes too long." As a solopreneur, now you've got my attention. I didn't know that people were bouncing off my website, and now that I know it, I want to hear how to fix it right now!

As a coach, your job is to educate people in your target market and help them understand problems that they're having that they don't even know exist. Then, you need to show them solutions to these issues. To do this, you must understand your Ideal Client really well. For example, when I started coaching real estate agents, I knew that they were doing old-school stuff like open houses, cold calling, and door-knocking because that's what they were taught to do. They were busting their buns and getting poor results. They didn't even know that there was a much easier, more effective way to market. They didn't understand the power of video, and the power of social media, and the power of marketing. They had never been taught to be marketers. The problem they had that they didn't know about was that they didn't know how to market properly, not only themselves but their listings as well. They needed to learn how to be marketers and how to make their marketing work for them. They needed it, but they didn't know it. My job was to explain the problem to them and show them that I had solutions for them.

Brainstorm about different problems your Ideal Client has, and solutions you could offer will help clarify your Big Revelation. You'll also uncover smaller problems they have and come up with solutions to them as well that you can use in content.

Triple Touchpoints for Maximum Impact

For your marketing campaign to be effective, you can't move too quickly. Some marketers are way too impatient and try to get people to give their contact information at the very first interaction. For example, they'll do a short video and then say, "For more great information on this topic, click here." After they click, the person will be asked for their contact info before they can see that "great information" you promised them. That's like asking someone to hop into the sack with you when you've only known them for 5 minutes. Odds are that you're not going to get lucky with that approach!

Instead, just like dating, people need to be coaxed along. They need to like and trust you. They need to feel comfortable with you and believe that you have what they're looking for and that you have their best interest at heart. I teach my students that they need at least three "touches" before asking for someone's information. With each "touch" or interaction with you, they are learning to trust and like you a little bit more.

The first "touch" might be a video on social media. This can be a video of tips or other information that your target market will find useful. You just give value and don't ask for anything in return, but you'll track the people who opened the video and watched it. Next, using targeted marketing (retargeting), you might send another video on a different topic to the people who watched the first one. This time, you might ask them to "click" to get another video or piece of information that is on a landing page or your website. If your first two videos really gave them value, they'll be encouraged to see what else you have up your sleeve. If they didn't get value from those first videos, they won't make that extra effort to click. They're self-selecting.

Next, you send another video with valuable information and ask them to click to another landing page, which is part of our funnel. This is your third "touch," so the time is right to ask for their information. They give us their information (so it's now there in the funnel), and we give them the good stuff they came for. Typically, you ask for their email and cell phone so they can get updates, your blog, or receive some kind of report or booklet. If you're coaching new moms, you might offer a free booklet on "Fast Weeknight Dinners." If you're coaching financial planners, you might offer a report on retirement funds that attract different age groups. If you're coaching chiropractors, you might offer your book on "How Chiropractors Can Serve More Clients Working Fewer Hours." Whatever you offer at this stage (and all the other stages), make sure it's something your market really needs and wants.

Throughout the entire sales funnel, your objective is to give them *real* value, something that will help solve their problems or make their lives better somehow. It can be information or tips and hacks.

It can be your insights into the industry or on a topic your program is geared toward. You are NOT trying to sell them! You are *serving* them. For some people, this is the hardest concept to truly get. Serve, don't sell. Serve, don't sell. (You may need to keep repeating it over and over to yourself until it sinks in.) Because the more you *serve*, the more you *will* sell!

For example, sending people an email that talks about how fantastic your tax filing software is would be *selling*. Sending people an email explaining how to take advantage of the latest changes in the tax code would be *serving* them. Creating a video that showcases your credentials as a real estate agent and how many homes you've sold would be *selling*. Creating a video that tells them what's going on in the market and how it might affect the sale of their home is *serving* them. Get the picture? If you've been in sales, this may be scary. But it's the approach that all the major brands are using, and it's much more effective than the old salesy model.

I mentioned Alex Hormozi (a well-known and respected marketer) in Chapter 5, where he said, "If you're not afraid that you're giving away too much, you aren't giving enough." You don't want to be thinking, *How little can I get away with?* when it comes to what you give potential customers for free. You want to make sure that everyone you touch, whether they end up signing up with you or not, has gained something valuable just by interacting with you. You want to make your free stuff better than what others are charging for.

When you serve rather than sell, you're building a relationship with them, especially if you're using video. You're positioning yourself as the expert and authority, gaining credibility. They begin to like you and trust you—and as a bonus, the ones who don't like you will disappear! But the ones who stay develop a positive relationship with you that will eventually get them to sign up with you. But don't get impatient! It's probably the number one mistake people make! You want to give them 3 "touches" where you've gifted them with something of value before you *ever* ask for anything in return. If you rush them, they don't have time to learn to trust you and like you. They can't yet see that you have their best interests at heart. They'll still be suspicious of you and hesitant to move forward. So be patient. This strategy works so well that Russell Brunson (CEO of ClickFunnels who is an amazing marketer) had me speak at Funnel Hacking Live in front of around 5,000 people about the "Pre-Funnel" and what you do before driving traffic to your funnel.

Now, let's say that your Ideal Client is a dentist who is looking to make more money in her business. You might start your funnel with a video titled "5 Biggest Money Mistakes Dentists Make." Next, for the people who pay attention to that video, you could retarget them with a video on "Hiring the Best People for Your Dental Practice." After that, you could have them click on a landing page and give them a report on "Where Dentistry is Heading and How to Get Ahead of the Trends." Or if you've written a book on "Secrets of a Super Successful Dentist," you could give them a digital version.

This is where you'll ask for their information to give them the Secrets book or the report on trends. Keep in mind that the more things you ask for in terms of their contact information, the more likely they will not give it to you. Just ask for what you need. Email and first name are a must, but you don't necessarily need their last name. If you are going to ask for a phone number, don't make it mandatory. Make it optional and give them reasons why they might want to provide it. For example, "to be listed in a drawing," "to get reminders," "to make sure you don't miss out on special offers," etc. I'm not an attorney, so when you get their contact information, make sure you are following privacy laws about calling or contacting them.

In the Million Dollar Month Model, the next stage is to invite them to a free webinar. (However, as I mentioned before, if your 3-day Event is happening in the next day or two, you invite them to that instead.) You can either do a free 90-minute session or the hour-long sessions for five days that I used to do. Most presenters call these "challenges," and I've seen all kinds. Before we started doing the 90-minute webinar, a challenge that lasted five days for one hour per day was our sweet spot. But our 90-minute *What's Working Now* webinar is even better. During this free training (5-day challenge), you teach them something that will *really, truly* improve their lives or their business. It's not just a glorified sales pitch. Serve, don't sell!

During the free session (either 90-minute webinar or 5-days), you'll invite them to participate in your longer 2-3 day training event that is at a low cost, usually $47 to $97. Again, what you teach during this 2-3 day event has to be totally worth the time they're putting into it! Within this event, you'll give them the chance to sign up for your full-blown coaching program.

Broken down simply, it looks like this:

- Video
- Video
- High-value resource on landing page in your funnel (pdf, report, book, video series training, etc.)
- Free Webinar (90-minute or 5-day)
- Low-cost virtual event (2-3 day)

Creating Your Winning MDMM Marketing Campaign

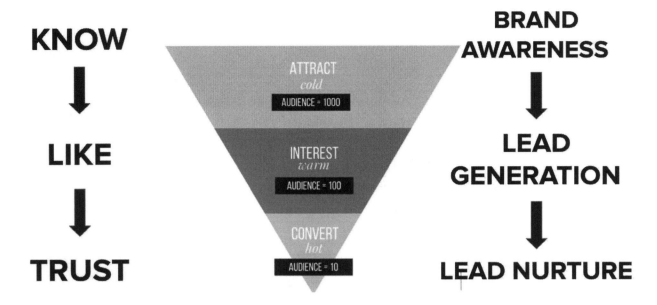

One of the basics of effective digital marketing in the 21st century is to use sales funnels. Sales funnels are automated, so once you set them up and populate them with lead magnets—videos, articles, "free reviews"—your funnels will be marketing for you while you sleep! There are various companies out there with software that automates funnels. We've developed software of our own called the Mashore Method to capture all the tracking and different options that, from my experience, are important to have.

The idea of a sales funnel is very simple. You start marketing online to a large group of people, then narrow it down in stages until you end up with the people who are your most likely customers. At the top of your funnel, you have a broad range of potential clients. You offer these people value in some form, track the people who express interest in what you've offered, and offer those people even more value. As you do this, people will self-select in and out. Your funnel will narrow as you go, and you'll end up with a smaller number of people at the bottom who are your most likely new clients. You keep offering them value until they're hooked and ready to sign up.

The important thing to recognize with an actual funnel (like a funnel in the ClickFunnels software or a funnel in the Mashore Method software) is that when you direct traffic to a specific funnel, it is for one specific purpose. You've targeted people, and they showed interest in the material you put in front of them. So, you know that they ended up in that funnel because they are interested in what you have to offer. The software makes sure that everything in that funnel is specific to the exact content they are interested in. This is different than a website because on a website, you don't know why they are there. Are they looking for reviews? Are they trying to learn more about you? You just can't be sure why they land on your website. A funnel is much more directed.

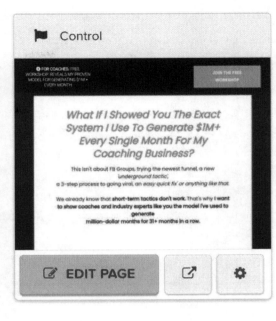

Filling Up Your 3-Day Event

As I talked about earlier, on the third touch of your campaign, you start driving traffic to your free webinars (or free 5-day challenge) and then drive them to your 2-3 day virtual event. In this step, you create engaging content and then offer them a high-value resource on the landing page in your funnel (like a pdf/report/ book/video series training) that they opt-in to get.

Next, you will retarget the people who opt-in to go to either the webinar or the 3-day event, depending on what is next on the calendar. We direct traffic to the webinar if that is the next thing up or the 3-day if that comes sooner. We have found there is no difference in conversion if they do go to the webinar first or if they go directly to the 3-day event. However, we still do a free webinar so that we get more opt-ins and have another opportunity to invite people to the 3-day.

To get to one million dollars per month, how many leads do you need to start with? The short answer is, "More than you think." To get more accurate about the number of leads you need, you can use a Money to Math calculator. Start with how much money you want to make in a month. To keep it simple, let's say you want to gross $100,000 per month, and the program you offer is $10,000. That means you need just ten people to sign up for your program each month.

And let's say you start with 1,000 leads and that they are qualified leads (meaning they really could use what you offer). Out of those 1,000 leads, maybe 720 will decide to join your free webinar. Industry statistics say that only 10-25% of the people who opt-in for a free webinar will show up. Let's say that 75% will be no-shows, so you might end up with 180. At the free webinar, you'll offer your 180 people the opportunity to attend your low-cost, 2-3 day virtual event. If you've given them terrific value during the webinar, you might get 50 people who choose to go for it and 45 who actually show up for it. You'll offer your full coaching program on Day 2 (before lunch) and Day 3 (after lunch) of your 3-day virtual event (by then, you'll probably have 35 still in attendance). How many of those will sign up for your program? All of this depends on your conversion rates as you go along. Now that I've been doing this for a while, mine are pretty good. (To see a spreadsheet of my conversion rates and everything we track to optimize, go to Theprovenmodel.com/resources.)

Scan this QR code using the camera app on your phone to access your resource page & added freebies now!

So you can see that starting with plenty of qualified leads is key to making this happen! Where do you find them? For our first few events, we filled it organically, and we had higher conversions because these people were fans and followers. Over time, we shifted toward paid leads who hadn't been nurtured as long.

As I mentioned before, one common false belief many of my MDMM students have is that they have to have a huge list in order to make an impact. They think that they need to be super influential already. They think that they have to have all of these accolades and stats in order to do well, and the point is they just need to be one or two steps ahead of the people they're trying to serve. Yes, to do a million-dollar month, you'll need a large audience. But you could do $175,000 a month with 35 people seeing your offer. One of my first students, Shauna, did just that. She didn't have a huge list, and there was some kind of glitch in their Facebook advertising, so she ended up having just 35 people at her very first 3-day virtual event. But you know what? Out of that group, six people enrolled in her program at $25,000 each! Then, she got another person enrolled during the follow-up to the event. At his first 3-day event, my student Tim only had 30 people. Out of those 30, he enrolled six for a total of $103,000! In his second month, Tim had 24 people show up, and 21 people stayed to see his offer. He sold five this time for $125,000. Tiffany had 57 people by the time she made her offer during her first 3-day event. Of those, eight people signed up, which brought in $143,976. Another student, Phil, spent only $38,000 in ad spend, had 84 attendees, and brought in $250,000 in a 4-month period. It's just a matter of doing it the right way. These students knew very clearly what their Ideal Clients wanted and gave it to them while helping them believe that they could be successful.

I didn't start with a huge list either, though now, of course, it's grown. But one thing that makes my list powerful is that they are *engaged* with me. You can have a list with thousands of names, but if you haven't really connected with them, you won't get much in results. To engage and connect, you have to really know your Ideal Client inside and out, then give them what they need and want. When you do that, you'll find that a smaller, much more engaged list is much more impactful than just big numbers.

Filling Up Your Webinar

Start in the most obvious place: your email list. You want to send your email list great videos with valuable content that they can use. For some of these, you can just add a banner at the end with some graphics and info about your webinar (then later, you'll highlight your 2-3 day event). For others, you can do a subtle promo for the webinar at the end of your video. Just make sure that you're giving them great content first. And remember to always promote whichever is next, the webinar or the 3-day event. The reason this is so important is that the longer away a training is, the more no-shows you will get. You want to promote the training that is soonest so you get more people to attend. It's easy to be excited about something and sign up. But the farther away it is, the excitement fades, and often, they forget what it's about and why they wanted to attend. So, they just won't show up.

In all your marketing, pay attention to the emails that get opened and the videos that get watched. Notice the headlines that people seem to open more than others when you run ads and keep track of what emails and headlines work. At times, you'll notice that people get ad fatigue on a certain headline or topic. Pull it for a while, but more often than not, once you take it down for a while, if it worked once, it will work again in the future. The emails that are opened are the ones that are engaging to your audience. You can then send that engaged audience into your funnel for more content. These are the people you can promote to personally.

Can you keep promoting your monthly webinars to your email list every month? Yes! Keep giving them great content. If they didn't attend the webinar before, you can say, "You missed a great session, but we've got a new one coming!" You can let them know anytime you change it up, when you've added new content to the webinar, or when you have a special guest coming.

You can also provide a great, valuable training for someone else's audience, a group you also want to attract. For example, a divorce attorney may be a good person for a real estate agent to connect with. Someone who does yoga trainings might pair up with a nutrition coach. If you can offer a great, valuable training to their clients, you can get closer to their list.

At the same time, you should be generating leads from social media, using whatever platforms your Ideal Client would be on. You can do video posts or stories. You can do Facebook Lives and livestream into groups as a teaser. You can use lead magnets like reports, or checklists, or tips to get people to message you and your team. Through those, you can keep nurturing them with useful information as you promote your event. I always tell my students, *"When you are promoting an event, all roads lead to the virtual event."* Everything you do or give them should be directing the traffic to the event. You shouldn't have a bunch of offers that you are marketing all at the same time. It just confuses people.

Also, run some paid ads on social media. Don't be afraid to spend some money here. Think about it: If you get just one new client from an ad, how much is that worth to you? By the way, the most effective ads are ads that don't look like ads at all. Your goal is to get people to "stop the scroll" when they are on social media. If something looks salesy, people are more likely to just scroll past it. You've got to capture their attention without seeming like you're trying to only sell them something.

For example, one of my students told me that her best-performing ad was a short video that featured her little daughter doing something funny that related to her business. She knew that her Ideal Client would stop scrolling to get a little laugh and watch a cute kid. I've used a picture of somebody who's got her head on the desk crying and throwing a phone down because she's been doing so much cold calling. My Ideal Clients can immediately relate. Then, when they click on the ad, it takes them to the page that tells them that they can succeed much faster without all that cold calling. You can use anything, like a beautiful picture, an unusual photo, or a funny meme, to make your point. Just think about what your Ideal Client would be into and what would catch their attention.

For MDMM, I use a picture of me with all of my ClickFunnel awards behind me. That really stops the scroll because the people I'm trying to attract typically know exactly what those are and what they mean. They see 11 plaques for Two-Comma Club Awards, two plaques for 10x Awards, and two plaques for $25 Million Awards. That stops them right in their tracks, and they watch my content because they then know I'm the real deal. In fact, almost ALL of them tell my sales team that they saw all my awards and knew that I'd achieved that level of success.

Filling Your 2-3 Day Virtual Event

You'll do many of the same things you did for your webinar to promote your 2-3 day virtual event—but you won't promote both at the same time! We found out that it just confuses people to hear about two different trainings at the same time. Once the webinar was over, then you'd drive traffic to the 3-day. In MDMM, we schedule the webinar and then a 3-day event two weeks later. Send them to whatever is next on the calendar.

If you try to market either the webinar or 3-day event more than 14 days ahead of time, we notice that more people don't show up, and our conversion rates also go down. So, zero to 10 days prior to the webinar, you'll market the webinar. Then, ten days prior to the 3-day virtual training, you'll drive traffic to that. And don't forget, the webinar's offer is to attend the virtual 3-day training, not your full program.

When the webinar is over, you can do a "replay" campaign. Send a link to the replay to anyone who signed up but didn't show up. Send the link to people who showed interest but didn't sign up. Promote a watch party for the replay on Facebook and do daily livestreams in Facebook groups. Do more ads with clips from the webinar. But I wouldn't recommend doing replays of the 3-day virtual event. You want them to show up and attend as much as possible. We tell them that we don't give recordings (unless they bought our $297.00 upsell for the recordings) because then they think they don't have to attend. They think they can just watch the recording later, but they never actually end up watching it. Also, if they have the recordings, they may say, "I've got the recordings. I'll just try to figure this all out on my own and maybe buy later." Giving recordings can (and, in my opinion, will) cause conversions to go down and no-shows to go up. So right now, we are exploring other things to upsell (because upsells help counteract ad cost) that are NOT recordings and removing that option altogether.

MDMM Mindset: GETMO

One of the most important mindsets you can adopt in starting your MDMM coaching business is GETMO: Good Enough To Move On! Too many people wait for everything to be perfect. Your business, your program, and your marketing will all evolve and get better. But don't wait for "better" and certainly don't wait for "perfect"! You can't make something better if you haven't *experienced* what's working and what's not. By starting, you get to see the areas that need improvement. *Starting* and *doing* is how you'll learn to make it better, not just sitting back and thinking about it. Just get out there and get started. Yes, you'll make some mistakes, but don't let it stop you from starting.

Too many people waste so much time getting their ducks in a row. Have you ever seen a row of ducks? They aren't perfect. They wobble all over the place, and so will you. I always say, "Ready, Aim, Fire!!" I always see people Getting Ready and Aiming but never Firing. Fire, Fire, Fire more! If you spend too much time worrying about making it all perfect, odds are that you'll never start at all. So, just get Good Enough to Move On in *everything* you do for your business. GETMO to get mo' money!

Final Word

If you've gotten to this point and have read through the whole book, then you have just about all you need to get started building your own Million Dollar Month Model business. I'm guessing you're like my MDMM students when they first start out: a little bit excited and a little bit scared—or maybe a lot scared! You're afraid you don't have a big enough list. You're afraid it's going to take too much time. You're afraid you don't know what to talk about. You're afraid nobody's going to listen to you. You're thinking, *Who the heck am I to be a coach or have a high ticket offer?*

It may all feel like a big, beautiful dream to you. Dreaming big is good, but dreaming alone won't get you where you want to go. You have to take action *even while you're scared*. That's when you get all the rewards. I know this personally. Most everything I've done to build my businesses has been scary to me. Taking action even while my knees were shaking has gotten me where I am today. Let me give you a recent example.

In 2022, Tony Robbins and Dean Graziosi were launching a program using a 5-day challenge. It was literally the largest affiliate launch in the world at that time—and I was asked to join it!

An affiliate launch is when someone asks others (affiliates) to promote their product or service. You team up with them to promote their product either because you just want to do them a favor or you really believe in their product, or because you get paid some kind of commission. I had never done one before—and I was starting with what was the largest affiliate launch *ever* at that time! To say I was afraid would be a huge understatement! I was terrified!

See, I would be competing against people who had millions of followers, people like Ed Mylett, Brendon Burchard, Tom Bilyeu, and Russell Brunson. As my fear was happy to point out, I'd literally be competing with people who would be almost impossible to beat! They all have millions of followers and people on their email lists. Me? I had a list of about 30,000 active people who opened up my emails. In fact, many of the people who I would be competing against were so well-known that they were actually featured in the training program we were promoting!

My fear kept saying, *What makes you think...What are you doing?... You aren't in their league... There's no way that you're going to be able to beat Russell Brunson.* For God's sake, he is my mentor. I know he has millions of followers. He has huge influence. He has a personal friendship with Tony Robbins and Dean Graziosi. That's how high up the chain these people are that I'm competing against. I knew I had to really completely change my mindset. I had to remember my *why*. I had to just visualize what I wanted and stop thinking about all the obstacles.

I gave myself a good talking to: "It *is* possible. You have a really strong influence, and you love your people, and you would never do anything you don't believe in. This program will really help and support them. By winning this launch challenge, you'll get to be in the room with some amazing people. So, just keep believing that this can happen. Just do it."

I had checked out the program they wanted me to promote to make sure it would actually be good for my students. I wasn't going to do this just because it would be so great for me and my career. It had to benefit my students as well. Being of service to others is another of my strong values. So, I went through the first half of the program, and OMG! It was awesome! It was so aligned with what I teach. They had brought in trainers and teachers for this program that I had literally spent hundreds of thousands of dollars to get coaching from. Russell Brunson was teaching in the course, and I've paid him over $400,000. Alex Hormozi was in the course, and I'd paid him $25,000 for just eight hours of coaching me. I mean, the people in the program are amazing trainers and coaches —not to mention Tony and Dean. So, I thought, *This is awesome!* I called and said, "Yes. Absolutely, I'm in!"

I also knew that doing this would be really, really good for my brand in personal development and business coaching and consulting. Tony Robbins has been in the personal development space for around 45 years, and I think Dean's done it for 20 or more. In this launch challenge, the top ten affiliates would get to go to a 5-day mastermind with Tony, Dean, and the other top affiliates. That alone, that experience of being around those kinds of marketing brains and people that have achieved such greatness, was incredible. Wouldn't you pay a million bucks just to be a fly in the room with Tony and Dean?

I kept using all the mindset techniques I wrote about in my book, *Stop, Snap & Switch: Train Your Brain to Unleash Your Limitless Life*. I started visualizing myself at a long rectangular table with Tony and Dean. Tony is at the head of the table, and his wife is to the right of him. I'm next to her, and my husband, Steve, is next to me. Dean and his wife are across from us, and Russell Brunson and his wife are next to them. It's weird because my visualizations have never been as vivid as this one was! I could feel it and taste it. I literally was *at* the mastermind. I just kept seeing it, and I kept believing. I quit saying I couldn't do it and started saying, "I'm doing it!"

Even so, I have to confess to you that almost every single day during the launch, I'd panic, even if it was just for a moment or two. This was bigger than just about anything I had ever done! I was getting emotional whiplash from feeling positive and excited one minute to needing to Stop, Snap and Switch from some crazy negative thought. Even after years of working on this stuff and strengthening my mindset, a bigger challenge always calls up bigger fears. But I knew that fear was just rearing its ugly head again. So, I kept believing, and visualizing, and taking action.

I made a big mistake at first (one of several that I'm going to share with you). At first, I was just trying to get into the top 10, and quite honestly, it seemed like a huge stretch even to get in the top 10. There are two phases to the launch challenge. The first phase is to see how many people you can encourage to sign up for the free 5-days of teaching. The second phase is to see how many of your people actually buy into the program. I should have been focusing on being in the top ten of that *first* phase first. By the time that first phase ended, I was number 14 based on the number of people I had brought to the free session.

I looked at that, and my first thought (from listening to my fear, of course!) *So, there's no way I can get to the top 10 in the second phase from here! Just look at the math.* **How** *am I ever going to do it?*

And suddenly, I realized I was asking the wrong question. "How" will always mess you up. You need to be asking "why," not "how." With a strong enough why, you'll always figure out a "how." I had to stop asking "how" because when I asked "how," it seemed almost too impossible. I had to just make the commitment to do it and just do it. So, I told my fear to take a hike, and I kept visualizing *what* I wanted and *why* I wanted it. And as I did, I came up with more ideas for how to do it. And when the second phase of people buying the program started, the one that really counted, I was at number ONE on the leaderboard! I was so excited!

But that's when I made another mistake. I kept visualizing myself as number *two* because, doing the math and looking at it logically, I didn't think there was any way in the world I'd be able to beat Russell Brunson and a few of the other heavy hitters who had millions of followers and a huge email list. I was number one for a little over two days, and then all of a sudden, Russell Brunson went up to number one and stayed there for a couple of days!

I caught myself and thought, *Krista, he's number one because you've been visualizing yourself as number two. You've got to visualize yourself as number one!* I did, and literally, Russell and I went back and forth for about a day and a half. Russell was in the lead, then I was in the lead, then Russell was in the lead. Then, after a day or so, I remained in first place until the last 8-10 hours! I was beating Russell! Then what happens? The next thing you know, this guy named Corby shoots to the top and ends up staying at number one and winning the challenge! (I found out later that he had to join forces with another guy in the top ten during phase one because they figured it was the only way they could beat me!)

Was I disappointed? Well, maybe a little. I'm human, after all! But the fact that I took second place is almost unbelievable. It doesn't make sense that I would be able to compete with people with millions and millions of followers on social channels. They have huge email lists. They're all influencers. For example, Ed Mylett has one of the largest podcasts in the world on marketing. And I realized that the reason I beat almost all of them is because I've offered so much value to my students over the years. I've helped and supported them. They trust me, so I was able to influence and persuade them in an ethical way to do something that I absolutely believed would help them. My list was much, much smaller, but my leads were actually stronger because of the trust they have in me. And *that* makes me feel awesome!

When I found out I was number two, I celebrated how far I'd come, from "This is impossible" to "I did it!" I had used every trick in my mindset playbook—not letting my fear run the show, ignoring the how and finding my why, affirming and visualizing what I wanted, making mistakes and correcting them, and an attitude of service—and that had taken me farther than I thought I could ever go.

When you have a dream or goal, you've got to believe in it, and you've got to see it, and you've got to visualize it, and you've got to keep visualizing it. You can't let your fear determine your destiny. I have to tell you, the mental struggle that I had in my brain during that two-week time frame was crazy! "Why are you doing this? You shouldn't be doing this. What makes you think you can win? There's no way you're going to be able to win." I had to constantly Stop, Snap and Switch (the technique I showed you in Chapter 4). I had to Stop, Snap and *Do* rather than worry. I had to Stop, Snap and *Believe* that I could do it. I had to Stop, Snap and *Remember* times I'd overcome the odds before. I had to Stop, Snap and *Visualize* what I wanted.

I just did it and worked past my fear and doubt, my fear of losing, my fears that made me feel inadequate. I just took action, right? And because of that, I not only got to be at the retreat I had been visualizing, I've gotten to develop a relationship with Dean. He called me on Wednesday recently because the trainer for their mastermind had canceled suddenly, and they needed someone by Friday. So, again, I took action. I said "Yes" quickly, changed my schedule around, and didn't second guess myself. They flew me to the studio in Phoenix, and I gave the mindset training for that month.

Afterward, Dean thanked me, and then I got really bold and gutsy. "Dean, I'm like your Ideal Client, right? I understand how important it is to have somebody on stage that your Ideal Client can relate to. Don't you think it might help you to have me on your stage either at your next challenge or at one of your events?" He said, "You know, you're right." And for their 2023 challenge, Dean and Tony invited me to be one of the speakers that had over a million people registered.

What if I had bought into my fear of self-doubt, of not feeling worthy enough and not good enough to compete with those people in the 2022 challenge? None of these other opportunities would have opened up. I took some really uncomfortable, scary actions, and I acted quickly. Action-takers are money makers. Money likes speed. You have to just say "yes" and just do it.

Now, all these opportunities are opening up, and I'm reaching a goal that I set six years ago: to speak on Tony Robbins' stage. It took me six years to get on that stage and a ton of work, and time, and money, and energy, and failure, and resources. But you just can't give up, and you can't listen to your fears.

One of my students, Tiffany, told me the story of her first couple of months working on her MDMM business. "Krista and her team were very supportive and motivating. And when I left after that first session, she said to me, 'Just say yes to yourself. There's a saying that if somebody makes more money than you, you should do what they do. And when you make more money than them, they'll do what you do. You're smart; you have the *it* factor.' She pumped me up, and when I left and was driving on the freeway, I saw this huge rainbow, and it was like you could almost see where the pot of gold would be."

"A couple of months later, I was going through hell. I was trying to learn all these things, creating the slides for my event, and building my MDMM team. I had never done anything like this before. I would be crying and afraid, then laughing and being so excited, then crying again. Then, one day, I saw a post from Mel Robbins: 'Everybody wants the rainbow and the pot of gold at the end, but they don't want to walk through the bad weather and be in the rain.' And it hit me like a ton of bricks. That's why I saw that rainbow."

You can't get to the rainbow and the pot of gold without walking (taking action) through the rain (your fears).

The Heart of an MDMM Business

One of the main reasons I decided to teach others the Million Dollar Month Model is that I want to expand my reach exponentially and help people. And I know I can do this by helping other coaches and those with terrific high-ticket offers to expand their reach. They'll be able to reach people that I can't. Yes, I want to help my MDMM students make more money from their business. But it's important to me that they are really in it to serve people like I am.

There are tons of coaches out there these days. I think most of them have good intentions, though I'm guessing some people get into it because they think it's easy. Some of these coaches are good, some are horrible, and some are just meh. But very, very few coaches are Million Dollar Month Coaches.

The ones I've learned from, like Tony Robbins, Dean Graziosi, Jason Fladlien, Russell Brunson, are very different from each other in many ways. But I think it's their basic principles and values that have allowed them to build Million Dollar Month coaching businesses. I'm guessing that, just like the success principles that Napoleon Hill talks about, not all of these coaches were born with the principles of a Million Dollar Coach or MDMM offer. They learned them. And you can learn them, too. Here are some of the principles I believe in.

Teach More Than You're Teaching

I know that looks like a typo. But I heard an interview with John Wooden recently, one of the most successful college basketball coaches ever, and he was asked what a coach is. He said that a coach is essentially a teacher and that, as a coach, your job is to teach your particular subject and inspire your students to be the best they can be in that subject. It's not to make sure they all get A's or win trophies or win contests. It's about teaching them and encouraging them to give it their all in *whatever* you're teaching. And when you do that, you're teaching them how to live a successful life, not just how to be a great basketball player or how to ace the SAT to get into a great college.

That's so important. No matter what the subject of your coaching is, to me a Million Dollar Coach doesn't just show their students how to have more lucrative accounting businesses or how to create a home-based business with great cash flow. A Million Dollar Coach helps students improve their lives in all areas: how they feel about themselves, their relationships, their family, their business, their physical and mental health. That's real abundance, real success.

We've gotten used to judging success by money alone. Don't get me wrong. I want my students to be able to make as much money as they want to. But I also know that you can have all the money in the world and still not be happy or fulfilled. If you're miserable and not happy, if you're not enjoying your life and yourself and your family, it doesn't matter how much money you make. And the truth is, I've found that it's so much easier to make money when you have a happier life. The happier you are, the better life you have, and the more you appreciate it, the money just starts to come. It's much, much easier to do what you need to do without stress and misery dragging you down.

Even if your program doesn't have to do with helping people be more financially successful, this idea is still true. When John Wooden coached his college athletes, he wasn't just focused on making them better basketball players. He knew that when they left college, most of them would leave basketball behind. So, he wanted to make sure that they were growing into responsible young men who knew how to work hard for what they wanted and had values that would give them a fulfilling life. In Coach Wooden's interview, he talked about another well-known coach, Amos Alonzo Stagg. Coach Stagg's team had just had an incredible season, and a journalist said, "So, you must feel like your coaching was really successful this year." Coach Stagg said, "Well, I won't really know how successful for another 20 years."

As a Million Dollar Coach, this needs to be one of the qualities you adopt: *To coach people so that they have abundance and success in all areas of their lives, not just the area you're teaching.*

Give More Than You Expect to Get

For many years, I've taught, "Serve, don't sell. Put people before things, and the things will come." That's always been key for me. And as I was thinking about starting my coaching business and studying what great coaches were doing, I saw that they were crazy committed to serving their clients and students. They focused on giving incredible value and getting great results for people. They bent over backward to give students what they needed and make them feel special and respected. I paid some of these coaches mega-bucks to help me along the way, and (with just a couple of exceptions) I always felt that I got *much more* than my money's worth. Some people worry that if they give "too much," they won't succeed. Based on my own business and the great Million Dollar Coaches I've known, that just isn't true.

Now, I'm not saying this is right or wrong, but in the first couple of years in my coaching business, I didn't make tons of money because I kept putting money back into the business. I'm so obsessed with the client experience and the client results. Even when I was making almost nothing, I wanted my students to have a Million Dollar Coaching experience. I put money into systems. I put money into support staff, into my accountability coaches, and our office hours. I put money into anything that I thought would give more value to my clients.

I was also in the beginning learning phase. If you look at my coaching program that I have now, it's 95% better than it was in the beginning. It was great back then, with incredible information and strategies. But with experience, I started learning what people truly need to help them be successful. And whenever I learned something that I thought would make a real difference to my students, I added it.

Make It About Them, Not You

Students come to you because they need help to get where they want to go. Your job is to show them *how* to get where they want to go, not to tell them *where* they should go. Everyone's definition of success is different. To you, a happy marriage might be that you and your partner have a crazy great sex life, experience ongoing personal growth together, and share adventures in life. To one of your clients, a great marriage might have more to do with trust and stability. When I was actively in real estate, my definition of success was selling at least 100 homes per year, but many of my students only want to get to 20 homes per year. I make sure that they don't feel like their goal isn't valid. For me personally, my coaching business is successful if it helps my students succeed and it generates more than $1M per month. But some of my MDMM clients see success as $200,000 per month, and that's great. Our job as MDMM coaches is not to push our idea of success on them but to help them achieve *their* definition of success.

That said, we do want to inspire them to think bigger than they've been thinking. Maybe their goal was a marriage that was stable because they didn't think an exciting marriage was possible. Maybe their goal was to sell 20 houses per year because they didn't think they could sell 100. Maybe they thought a $200k per month coaching business was all that was possible for them. Our job is to encourage them to reach farther than their limited thinking tells them that they can reach.

The key here is to *inspire* them without making them feel like they're inadequate. I do that by constantly showing them success stories, and I tell them that the reason I do it is so they can say, "I'm next! That can be me!" ***I teach them to celebrate and be proud of all their small wins and to absolutely avoid comparing themselves to others.*** We also give awards for achievement at different levels.

Constant and Never Ending Improvement

This is huge! You need to keep adapting and growing to make your coaching calls, your coaches, your customer service, and your training better. You have to constantly track what's working and what's not working for your students and make changes as necessary. You need to focus on how you can help people be successful, not just focus on landing them as a client. And that means taking some risks and trying things you haven't done before.

For example, very recently, I thought, *All I have are high ticket offers. The market is shifting, and people might need a lower price point. Maybe I should try what others have suggested and offer a lower ticket offer.* I figured that if I can sell $24,000 programs, it should be easy to sell a $2,000 program. So, I did a webinar, and about 203 people attended—and then I had the worst close ratio ever! I only had one sale (though we sold two more in our follow-up). But I didn't give up. I hired someone to get better at creating webinars, and I redid it the next week. We had 277 this time, and the webinar was killer. Then, when I went to make my offer, my slides went blank for literally 15 minutes! I couldn't find them. It was the biggest #*%! show ever! Finally, I realized I was clicking the wrong slides, but by then, I had already lost 143 people. So, only 134 saw the offer. I still sold 28 of my $2,000 packages. But again, I'd learned something, so I did the webinar again the very next day. And we're still working to improve it. It's very different from my Million Dollar Month Model, and it's new to me. So, I have to expect a learning curve.

One thing I know for sure is that if you don't start at something new, you won't get better. Number two, if you don't keep going, you aren't going to get better. You have to keep going and keep trying even though at first, you aren't very good. You need to constantly stay awake and aware regarding your students, what's working for them and what isn't, as well as new ideas and strategies that could help them succeed. You can't just create a program and then let it go on auto-pilot if you want a thriving, sustainable business.

A Final Final Word

If you have something awesome to offer the world (and we pretty much all do!), I hope I've been able to inspire you and encourage you. Building an MDMM business is not easy. But with all I've learned over the years and shared with you, you now definitely have a better foundation than I started with. The Million Dollar Month Model has worked for me and now has worked for my students. I know it can work for you once you decide and set your intention.

Wishing you great success—Krista

MDMM Mindset: Your Manifesto

A manifesto is a written declaration of your intentions, motives, commitments, and ultimate vision. It will not have every tiny detail of your MDMM coaching business. It will be short, no more than one page, and it will include all the important themes or ideas that are the basis of the business you want to create. It's based on your passion and purpose, your goals and your values. Think about your business, your main intentions for it, and the things that are most important to you. Then, come up with a sentence or two that gets to the heart of it for each area. Place this somewhere that you can see it and read it out loud every day to remind you of your vision. To see some examples of manifestos, go to Theprovenmodel.com/resources.

Scan this QR code using the camera app on your phone to access your resource page & added freebies now!

Thanks for reading *The Million Dollar Month Model*! Please consider leaving me a review by scanning the QR code below! I'd love to hear what you think!

Give *My Guide to Million Dollar Months* a 5-star review so that others who want to make a positive impact in the world are encouraged to learn what you're learning.

Be generous. When one of us succeeds, we all succeed.

Thank you!

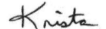